WHEN LIFE GIVES YOU LEMONS, MAKE WAFFLES

JIM NELSON

Publisher Information
Provision and Protection Publishing, LLC
2345 Twylby Rd
Larkspur, CO 80118

For more information or to contact the author, please email
Jim.PPP@bikerider.com.

ISBN 979-8-9985344-1-6 (softcover)
ISBN 979-8-9985344-0-9 (eBook)

Cover design: Terry Dugan
Cover photo credit:
    Waffle Illustration: INHE GAL@Adobe Stock
    Lemons Illustration: Hanna@Adobe Stock
Editorial team: Marcus Costantino, Claudia Volkman, Cristina Wright, and Amy Sinnott
Interior design: Ben Wolf, Inc.
Publishing services provided by BelieversBookServices.com

First printing: 2025
Printed in the United States of America

I dedicate this book to God Almighty, who is my provider and protector. I have not been able to find another plausible explanation for many of the events in my life, except through his grace and mercy.

CONTENTS

INTRODUCTION

"You can't handle the truth!"

In the explosive courtroom confrontation in *A Few Good Men*, Colonel Jessup (played by Jack Nicholson) delivers a searing statement in response to a bold demand made by the defense attorney Lieutenant Daniel Kaffee (played by Tom Cruise). As the colonel is on the witness stand, the tension mounts as holes in his testimony begin to appear—not everything he is saying under the penalty of perjury is true; worse, we are about to learn he believes the lies he is spewing.

With growing resentment toward the junior officer who is challenging his testimony, the colonel is confronted by a demand he is unready and unfit for, a demand for the truth. I can still feel the tension as the colonel yells into the courtroom, at war with the attorney.

"You want answers?"

"I think I'm entitled to answers!"

"You want answers?"

"I want the truth!"

"You can't handle the truth!"

It's not just a line—it's meant to expose the deep divide that exists between idealism and reality. Jessup's words reveal the raw, unvarnished truths of military life that he believes are too horrifying for civilian minds to grasp. He implies that the grim, morally ambiguous choices made in the name of national security are so brutal, so unforgiving, that they would shatter the carefully constructed illusions of those who have never faced such dark realities.

So, what about you and me and our lives? What illusions about life do we cling to? We'd like to think our journey will be problem-free, and that we will be spared any major tragedies. But the reality—the truth—is that no one escapes the pain and grief of life. The aching loss of loved ones, the disappointment of unfulfilled dreams, the disruption of natural disasters, the despair of job loss and financial instability, the burden of serious illness . . . these things are all part of our human experience.

The pages of this book tell the story of my journey through life. From surviving multiple traumatic brain injuries, career reversals, family issues, court trials, and more, I've had to drop any illusions I might have had and courageously seek the truth. And what I discovered in the midst of disappointment, despair, and discouragement is that hope and healing are available. God's goodness shows up when we need it most.

Some say, "God doesn't give us more than we can handle." I'm here to tell you that he does. And out of the mire of all the different things that have happened to me, I see more clearly than ever that God is still my provider and protector. This truth is bigger than any illusion that looms, and it transforms defeat into victory in amazing and surprising ways.

I've heard it said that people who often avoid thinking about matters of life and death will regularly embrace topics like heaven, hell, God, morality, and more when they are confronted with both beautiful and terrifying moments. We expect to hear about God's love and provision at weddings. We hope to hear about God's mercy and protection at funerals. I don't know about that. But what I can tell you is that when someone has a traumatic near-death experience, as I have, everyone stops to listen. Well, I have a story to tell, and I hope you listen.

Some of you already know about the events surrounding my bicycle accident on September 3, 2008. Maybe you heard about it on the news when it happened or after the court proceedings were completed. Maybe you and I have talked about it in a hospital, outside of a waiting room at an occupational therapy office, in the lobby at church, or while I was delivering your family waffles. Well, that accident and the years of recovery and litigation are just part of my story, just as any moment in your life is only part of yours.

When I woke up from my coma, I had lots of questions. Scratch that; I didn't have questions so much as I had a compulsion to breathe and live and fight. The questions came later. And the truth, later still. And the truth is that this life we live is beautifully frail. It is full of joy and sorrow; hope and heartache; love and sadness. Our lives, bodies, finances, and relationships are often frail. But there is still something beautiful in all of it.

While the many stories in this book are about my life, I promise to not make the book all about me. I want to join you in your story, in your days, in your hardships. I want to encourage you as we examine life together. I want you to keep your story in front of you even as you read about mine. Can you do that?

I'm also excited to introduce you to my friend Joe. We have shared a lot of life, and his story parallels mine in many ways. We have had many conversations throughout the years, and as I learned more about him, he became a companion on my journey, a trusted mentor I could turn to and converse with about my struggles. I want you to learn from him, just as I have. To that end, I'll share the nuggets of wisdom I've learned from Joe along the way. To get us started, one of the many things I have learned is that the way is not always easy, and it is rarely without its roadblocks, detours, potholes, or life-altering bicycle accidents.

I wish this were not so. I wish we could keep our jobs for as long as we desire them, that there would never be strife between us and our kids, and that not only would we always feel safe, but that we would be safe. I sure can relate to Colonel Jessup's perspective on how many of us think: "You don't want the truth because deep down in places you don't talk about at parties, you want me on that wall. You need me on that wall." Yes, we do want to feel safe, even if we have to pretend.

But no matter how hard we pretend, tragedy still strikes. And when it does, we have a choice: we can either become resentful or we can choose to live with hope. I choose hope. I choose to believe in the future. I choose to embrace the love of my wife, the goodness of God, and the joy of each day I have yet to live, even if the days behind me are full of pain and loss.

As I write, I'm mustering the courage to look deep into my life, and what I'm finding is that my life is worth living, and so is yours. Let's allow our lives to be intertwined for a bit, shall we? Let me share a bit of the truth I have discovered. Let me tell you what I have learned about life. Let me help you overcome loss and persevere toward the hope and healing you or someone in your life needs. I think you are worth it.

WAFFLES: A TICKET TO RIDE

The one who blesses others is abundantly blessed;
those who help others are helped.

There's something magical about watching a few simple ingredients transform into golden squares of comfort, one waffle at a time. As the waffle iron hisses to life, it fills the room with the rich aroma of melted butter and anticipation. Before the first bite, there's the quiet art of waiting—and the patience it takes to create the perfect waffle.

I've had a long history with waffles. In fact, making waffles was my ticket out of the hospital after the bike accident that forever changed my life, but my love for waffles started much earlier when I was a child.

I was born in Biloxi, Mississippi. My dad was in the Air Force, and my parents moved to California when I was only a year old. My parents were from northern Minnesota. Most of their families are still there, but my parents liked to move around. After being in California for a while, the company my dad was working for asked him to move to Utah for eighteen months. He said, "Sure, I'll go anywhere." We settled in Moab.

My parents were Christians, and I became a Christian at a

young age, but in Moab, we were the minority. There we were, in a Mormon state and a small town where most everyone was Mormon. Coming from California, that was a bit of a culture shock, to say the least.

Back to waffles . . . my mom had one of those old waffle irons, and we kids used to love it when she made waffles for us. Because she grew up without a family, Mom did everything she could to make our family life perfect. In her vision, that included a perfect Christmas Eve dinner and another beautiful meal on Christmas. However, when Christmas came around one year, she was too tired to cook another big meal. On Christmas Eve, she told my dad how tired she was, and she asked if he could take care of cooking on Christmas Day. My dad was no stranger to the kitchen, and he wanted to help my mom, so he agreed.

As he thought about it, he realized the fruit and nuts in our stockings would cover the breakfast meal, so he went to work figuring out another meal for the middle of the day. As he paged through the *Better Homes and Gardens Cookbook*, he saw it was pretty easy to make the waffle batter, so he decided he would figure out how to use the waffle iron. His efforts were successful —they were so good that waffles became a Christmas tradition. Over the years, Dad learned how to make a special topping called "Goodie." Similar to a luscious French topping, it consisted of separated eggs, sugar, and vanilla. With Mom's home-canned peaches, those waffles were even more delicious! Those are tastes and family experiences that will never be forgotten.

When I got married and had my own family, I continued the waffle-making tradition, though not always at Christmas. Sometime during the 1990s, I thought it would be a good idea to make the waffles a little more nutritious, so I started substituting ingredients. The results were just as good, and my waffle-making experiments continued.

Humble Beginnings and Hardy Stock

My heritage is one of hard work and persistence, and those values were handed down through the generations, and they continue to shape my life to this day. My grandfather was one of eleven children. He was raised on a productive dairy farm in southern Minnesota. After his parents died, though, things hit him hard. Since he was the only one in his family who wanted to continue farming, he paid off his siblings and took over owner-ship of the farm with a loan. Then a drought hit, followed by the Great Depression, and my grandfather lost virtually everything. He packed up all of his belongings and was able to buy a log cabin in the frozen swampland of northern Minnesota.

My grandfather was married by then, and during that time, my dad arrived on the scene. Life got even tougher, as he was born weak and sickly. My grandfather's family had experienced the death of other infants before, so they did not bother to name the new baby. As they struggled to do the best they could, Grandma and Grandpa decided to take him to Montana, leave him with his grandparents, and hope for the best. It proved to be a wise decision, and two years later, my dad was healthy and thriving. My grandparents went back to Montana and brought him home to Minnesota. That's when they finally named him James. One of the ironies in my dad's life is that, despite his diffi-cult beginnings, he has lived longer than anyone else in his family.

Dad grew up, joined the newly founded United States Air Force, moved to California, and then to Utah. One Easter morning in the late 1960s, he was taking my mom to a sunrise service outside of town when he was hit with a grand mal seizure while driving down Main Street. With this kind of neuro-logical attack, your body straightens and is stiff, and you lose consciousness. Obviously, it is not a good thing to do while driving. Fortunately, he survived, as did my mom.

Although it is hard to believe, during the next two decades, my dad experienced grand mal seizures two more times, both times when he was driving. Thankfully, no one else was injured when he seized while driving a carpool to work, or when his work truck went over a cliff. You can imagine the concern that having epilepsy can put on a man trying to provide for his family, but I don't ever recall him complaining about his condition. He just played the cards he was dealt. He just continued doing his best.

When I look back at these family events, it might appear from one perspective that I have inherited significant troubles from my dad and granddad. However, I don't look at it that way. They say farmers can fix anything. That's because back in the "old days," if you lived on a farm and something broke, your choice was either to figure out a way to fix it or go without food. I think that's why the people in Moab declared my dad to be the smartest man in town. He might not have been highly educated, but he could figure anything out.

Waffles to the Rescue

Fast-forward to 2008, after my bicycle accident. I was out of a coma and had been in the hospital for a month. The doctors were preparing to release me and wanted to be sure I would be able to function independently. My wife Elizabeth wanted this too—she didn't want to become the caregiver of an invalid along with her three young children. So, to demonstrate the level of my cognitive and functional skills, the doctors and my wife came up with a creative idea: "Let's have Jim make his waffles from scratch!"

I had to walk to the grocery store with an escort, select the ingredients, and purchase them. My wife brought the waffle iron to the hospital, and I had to demonstrate my ability to function cognitively by making waffles at the hospital. They might not have been the best waffles I'd ever made, but they were good enough that the hospital staff on the fifth floor enjoyed them, and the doctors approved my release.

My waffle-making didn't end there, though. I continued to experiment with different ingredients and came up with many delicious variations. I've been improving my waffles now for almost thirty years. I'm always trying to make my basic recipe better. And every time I try to make it a little bit healthier, it tastes better than before.

I love making waffles because it makes people happy. It started with my own family, but then I branched out and began making waffles as a way to let others know I cared. For instance, there's a family in our church that has six daughters, ranging in age from one to sixteen. Once in a while, I'll make a batch of waffles and bring it to their home, and they all love it.

A little while ago, our daughter texted me: "Mackenzie [our granddaughter] really wants some waffles." This is when she named my waffles "Papa Waffles!"

So, I'll make some Papa Waffles and take them to Mackenzie. Making waffles has become part of what I do. I love it because it shows my love for my family in a practical and delicious way. It never fails to bring back memories of my dad, too. There's just something about waffles!

In fact, there's even a book called *Men Are Like Waffles—Women Are Like Spaghetti* about how men's brains are like waffles![1] Now, we know men's and women's brains are different, but what makes a man's brain like a waffle? It's an interesting question, isn't it?

For one thing, just as a waffle is made up of small, separate squares, a man's brain also tends to be compartmentalized, with each box representing a different area of focus. Men like to stay

---

1. Bill and Pam Farrel, *Men Are Like Waffles—Women Are Like Spaghetti: Understanding and Delighting in Your Differences* (Eugene, OR: Harvest House Publishers, 2016).

in one box at a time, without mixing them up. They approach things in an orderly, logical fashion, one square at a time. As an engineer, I'm more of the waffle variety. Women, on the other hand, are more like spaghetti—their thoughts are interconnected; one idea leads to another in a nonlinear fashion.

Regardless of this metaphor, I've seen how waffles can be good conversation starters. When I returned home from the hospital, for the next year or two, I was disabled. I wasn't driving, so I'd go for a walk to the bank at the grocery store, which was a little over a mile away from our house.

At the bank (in the past I'd always used the ATM), since I had time, I'd go inside the bank and end up talking to the tellers and other people in the bank. Sometimes, the talk would turn to waffles. One day, someone recommended putting pumpkin in the waffle batter. I went home and experimented with this, and now fresh pumpkin waffles are one of my specialties.

My wife even suggested I start selling waffles since, over the years, I've come up with so many different variations that people really enjoy. My daughter in Tennessee has a son with a milk allergy, so I created a nondairy mix; and Elizabeth's daughter has a wheat allergy, so I had to come up with one that doesn't contain wheat. I've had about twenty different waffle irons—from a tiny one with a smiley face to the really big ones made in the 1950s. I bought an infrared thermometer so I could read the temperature and figure out the optimum setting (400 degrees). And how much batter does each waffle iron require? The small ones take one-fourth cup, and the bigger ones take up to a cup and a half. I discovered the only ladles that held a cup and a half were the ones used in restaurants, and I finally found one online. Who knew there were so many details involved in waffle-making?

I even consulted with a woman who has a small business that helps people in the food preparation industry. She walked me through the process of how to package my waffle mixes so they could be sold in stores. This opened my eyes to all it would take to get something like this off the ground, but for now, my wife and I have decided to put that idea on hold. However, God might not be done with this "waffle man"—so stay tuned!

And waffles aren't the only thing I make. As part of my healing journey, I've spent a lot of time in the kitchen. Especially during the first year after my accident, being disabled, I had time on my hands. One of the things I did with that time was cook. I enjoyed taking random ingredients, combining them with existing recipes, and making them into something new. Often, that meant substituting something on hand for something called for that we didn't have. After a while, I started writing these recipes down to keep track of what was good and what the kids liked.

So, while in general, I wouldn't say cooking is a great hobby of mine, I enjoy the creative aspects; it's fun to create something that others like, even if it is repetitious, like my waffles. When people like what I make, it adds to my enjoyment of giving. It turns out that different people have different tastes as well. In my continued quest to improve the flavor and healthiness of my waffles, over the years I have incorporated a variety of different ingredients: barley, oats, pumpkin, cocoa powder, blueberries, chocolate chips, bananas, strawberries, and even rhubarb and lemon.

During the first couple of years after the accident, I had been writing down various recipes that I came up with, and I decided to organize that information, including the box of random recipes I had previous to the accident. Being an engineer, I documented each recipe and included information about when it was developed, who liked it, and any idiosyncrasies due to cooking at altitude, etc.

When I finally was able to return to work, I mentioned my fascination with waffle-making and my collection of waffle recipes, and one of my coworkers recommended telling some of the story behind each recipe to add interest. When I did that, it added some personality, memories, and character, and pretty soon I realized I had a cookbook. I had copies printed as Christmas gifts for my family four years after the accident. I have also given copies to friends and colleagues who were interested.

I was reflecting on this recently with my friend Joe; he's someone who has gone through a lot and knows what it's like to trust God in the midst of heavy trials. He helped keep his family from starving during a severe famine, so he also knows how important food is when it comes to loving our families and those whom God puts in our path. I'll have more to say about Joe as this book unfolds. His story has helped me see God in my own story and make sense of it.

Do you have a specialty when it comes to cooking? In times of trouble, I can think of at least four ways a hobby like cooking can help.

1. It requires focus, which is why my wife and the medical team thought it would be a good test for me to see if I could navigate life on my own; it pulls you into the present moment, easing stress and anxiety.
2. It provides a sense of control—so valuable when life itself feels out of control.
3. It's a way to express creativity, which has certainly been true in my case as I've come up with lots of variations on the basic waffle.
4. It's a way to build connections with others and bond with family and friends, so it helps alleviate the feelings of isolation and loneliness that illness so often creates.

If you don't have a particular hobby, I highly recommend making waffles as something you might explore. And I'd be happy to share some of my best recipes with you.

2

EARLY LIFE LESSONS

Point your kids in the right direction —
when they're old they won't be lost.

Pop Bottles, Hubcaps, and Dumpster Diving

I f you were driving along a little-used road and noticed a pile of cash along the roadside, would you stop and pick it up, or would you continue on your way and let the wind blow it away? My guess is you'd be quick to stop your car and gather that cash before it was swept away. In a way, this is an example of how I learned to be a good steward from a very young age.

Starting in the late 1800s until the late 1960s, when you purchased something in a glass bottle, there was often a deposit associated with it. Consumers would pay the deposit and then return the bottles so they could be reused, which was much more efficient and economical than making new bottles. This also reduced the amount of trash and waste in our landfills. While this early recycling practice was good in theory, it is no longer practiced on that scale for a variety of reasons, primarily having to do with cost and efficiency as well as health and safety concerns.

My introduction to this philosophy came when, as young children, my sister and I learned that every pop (you might say "soda") bottle had a two-cent deposit associated with it. That was true whether we personally purchased the soft drink or not. So, if we found a pop bottle lying around anywhere, we could take it and return it to a store for a refund of the deposit. We learned this from our parents since that had been the case all of their lives as well.

This turned into an early income stream for my sister and me. When we were traveling in the car along the highway with our parents, we would watch the roadside, hoping to see a pop bottle that had been thrown out by another traveler. We would quickly tell Dad, "There's a pop bottle!" He would stop the car, and we would jump out and pick up the bottle we had spotted. Often, we would collect several bottles during a trip. When we got home, we would add these to our collection. We would wash the bottles with a garden hose, load them into our wagon, and take them to the nearby store to exchange them for the bottle deposits.

Each of us might end up with twenty-five cents or more. Even though things were much less expensive back then, we were not about to spend five or ten cents of our hard-earned money to buy a candy bar. We wanted to add this new cash to our savings, small as it may have been. We also never argued about who had collected the most bottles; we just split the profits equally.

Looking back, I realize this was an early lesson in both stewardship and multitasking—we were able to help clean up the roadside of debris that was not biodegradable and earn some income at the same time.

Years later, when I was living in Maryland, a similar opportunity arose. I discovered Hubcap City—a roadside business that sold used hubcaps. They had a large inventory, and they sold hubcaps more cheaply than it would cost to purchase them new from a car dealer. It turned out that they also purchased used hubcaps. I suppose, in today's culture, this would be a problem, as it might lead to hubcap theft, but that wasn't an issue back then. Often, hubcaps could be seen strewn along the roadway, where they had popped off a car's wheel when the driver hit a bump or pothole. To me, this seemed like a new, more profitable version of the pop bottle plan: pick up hubcaps from along the road and sell them to Hubcap City for cash.

By keeping an eye out for them, I regularly collected hubcaps, and once I had amassed a good amount, I'd head to Hubcap City and come away with a few bucks. Since my wife was from Connecticut, we often drove there from Maryland to visit relatives. One of the things I noticed on every trip was the great number of hubcaps lying along the roads in New Jersey and New York City. However, I certainly didn't want to risk the well-being of my wife and kids or take the time required to stop on these busy roads to collect hubcaps. But to me, this was like driving by piles of cash along the roadway.

At the time, my brother lived with us while he was attending trade school. He and I came up with a plan to do a hubcap run. We hopped in my Ford Ranger and drove from Baltimore to New York City. We left early on a Saturday morning when there was much less traffic, and our goal was to collect as many hubcaps as we could. We wanted to see how profitable it could be as a full-time business, or at least as a side hustle.

What we were doing wasn't illegal, but as you might imagine, it wasn't necessarily seen in a positive light by the police. Fortunately, we made it to New York City before we were stopped by an officer who advised us to discontinue our operations. By that time, we had filled the bed of my pickup, so we didn't have room to collect any more hubcaps anyway.

Our final analysis of that test run was that we probably earned the minimum wage for our time, and it paid for the gas for the trip. We decided it was a memorable but once-in-a-life-time experience.

Recently, we had a group of families over for a fall-fest barbeque and fellowship. During that event, when I was conversing with a couple of teenagers, one of them mentioned the term *dumpster diving*. Although it seems like a very deroga-tory term for a low-level practice, I shared with them the philos-ophy I have learned over these many years—that of good stewardship.

One definition of *stewardship* is that it refers to the position and duties of a steward, or the responsible overseeing and protection of something worth caring for and preserving. I believe we should be good stewards of the planet we have the privilege of living on. Although I may only have a very small role to play, each time I am able to reuse, refurbish, or recycle something, I have done something to help humankind be a better steward of this planet.

This concept of stewardship runs in my family. When I talked to my dad recently, he mentioned that he had taken some trash to the local dump. When I heard that, my first question was, "Did you come home with anything good?" His local dump has a process that allows you to take things that others are disposing of. As I suspected, on that day, they effectively traded their trash for some useful items. They were being good stewards.

What do you think when you see trash alongside the road? Do you shake your head and think it's a shame, or do you consider doing something about it? Do you feel it's up to the city or state to keep things clean? What if you thought about it as stewardship instead—a meaningful way you can make a differ-ence in your community and the environment? By choosing to get involved in cleanup efforts, you can help our world be cleaner, safer, and more beautiful.

I've found that participating in organized community cleanup events is a great way to get to know my neighbors and join together for a shared purpose. But even on my own, I continue my habit of looking for litter. It's not a big deal for me to carry disposable gloves and a trash bag during regular outings, whether I'm hiking on a trail, running on the beach, or walking through my neighborhood. By developing such a mind-set, we can all expand our concept of stewardship and know that we've made a difference, however small, in taking care of God's creation.

The Opposite of Teamwork

Teamwork is another concept that has been instilled in me, although my first experience of teamwork was less than positive. When I was ten years old, I joined Little League Baseball. I had no prior experience in sports—my dad never played sports when he was growing up, and he didn't play catch with me. We went fishing, and there were lots of other family activities, but baseball and other sports were things I didn't know much about.

My birthday is in October, and so I was always the youngest in my grade at school. I also wasn't very big for my age. Back in the 1960s, there were no rules like they have today about making sure every kid got to play. Consequently, for most of the season, I sat on the bench; the coach seldom put me in the game.

Our little mining town, Moab, was in the desert. Because of the heat, our games were always held in the evenings. On game day, there was a team rule that we couldn't go swimming during the day to conserve our energy for the game in the evening. Since I lived right across the street from the city pool, my usual day was filled with swimming all afternoon.

So, there I was on game day—I couldn't go swimming, which meant I couldn't have any fun, and then I had to go to the game and sit on the bench. Once in a while, the coach would put me in right field, where no balls ever got hit, and I'd stand around doing nothing, trying to look like I was there to do something.

One time, I finally got the opportunity to go up to bat. At that time, there was a "ten-run rule," meaning that if a team had a ten-point lead, they would stop the game no matter what inning it was and declare that team the winner. Well, when I got up to bat, we were winning by nine runs. The coach didn't want me up there because he was sure I would be struck out, and then the game would go for another inning. The coach pulled me out of the game and put another player in the batter's box in my place. We won the game, but I wasted my summer sitting on the bench.

Our team did so well that we were able to go to the state championship, which was quite an accomplishment for a little mining town that no one had ever heard of. It was a big deal—a four-day event in northern Utah.

That summer, my family had started attending a Baptist church in town, and the church's kids went to a summer camp each summer in Grand Mesa, Colorado—about a three-hour drive. It just so happened that the summer camp was being held on the same dates as the state Little League championship, so I had a choice to make. It was a pretty easy decision actually— would I go to the state championship and sit around and watch all my teammates play, or go to summer camp in a beautiful location? I didn't know much about the summer camp, but at least it would be something different, and I wouldn't be sitting around.

So, I went to summer camp that year—and that's when I first met God. One evening, there was a small group of us standing together, praying outside the chapel. The weather high in the mountains was pretty cool, but while we were praying, I felt an unusual warmth come over me. I believe it was the spirit of God filling me and warming me.

It made quite an impact on my dad when I got home and let him know I was saved. That led to a family baptism and a real change in our lives.

My next opportunity to get involved in sports followed a similar track, but it didn't result in a life-changing event.

On the back of our new house, my dad installed a basketball backboard and hoop so my sister and I could play on the patio. After a while, I got to be a pretty good shot, so early in seventh grade (the first year of junior high in those days), I decided to try out for the basketball team. I'd had a growth spurt by then, so I was one of the taller guys trying out for the team. As we were shooting hoops and practicing, I felt like I was doing pretty well and had good hopes of making the team when the coach had us all sit on the bleachers.

The next thing we had to do was write our names on a sheet of paper, with the position we wanted to play on the team. My challenge was that I had never watched a basketball game before, so I had no idea what the names of the positions were. I was so intimidated by my ignorance about the game that I didn't even write down my name—or ever again try out for another team.

While I never pursued team sports, I certainly learned the value of learning and being prepared ahead of time before trying something new. And I enjoyed plenty of other sports, such as bicycling, skiing, and trail riding. Cycling, in particular, brought me a lot of satisfaction and was a fun part of my fitness regime.

Back in the Day

People often talk about how life was "back in the good old days," but when I was young, I never thought that phrase might apply to me. Now, when I think about my early life, growing up in Moab, I realize the "good old days" are so much different from today in so many ways. Here are a variety of examples.

Back in those days, if you fell and hit your head and it hurt badly enough, doctors called it a concussion. Nowadays, if it's a more serious head injury, physicians use the more technical term *traumatic brain injury* or TBI. Since I seem to like to do things to the extreme, before I had an official TBI, I had my first concussion. When I was three or four years old, our family was living in southern California, and one day my mom and I were going to the hospital to check on my sister, who was there with pneumonia. As we backed out of the driveway and turned to go down the street, I realized I had forgotten my stuffed teddy bear. In those days, the car's front seat was a bench seat; there were no car seats or seat belts. So, when I wanted my teddy bear, I just pulled up on the door handle and opened the car door. Out I popped, landing on my head on the pavement.

My head hurt, but Mom just put me back in the car, and off we went to check on my sister. The next day, I started vomiting, and my parents realized I might have a concussion, so they took me to the doctor. It turned out that I did have a concussion, and I also had broken the back of my skull. To this day, I still have a big bump on the back of my head as a reminder. I am thankful I survived that event, and I realize why we now have seat belts, car seats for kids, and rules for them to not ride in the front seat.

Early Bicycle Adventures

Bicycles are very useful machines—both for fun and more utilitarian purposes. My love of bike riding started when I was quite young. I learned early on how to use them, and I also found ways to get injured with them. My first bike injury happened when I was in second grade. That's when I got my first bike and learned to ride it. Now, for a little kid, it was a pretty big bike; this was before they came out with the sporty bike style with a lower, longer seat. As I was riding in our neighborhood one day, I rode over a sloped curb. Unfortunately, there was some pea gravel on the curb that made my front wheel go sideways, throwing me to the sidewalk.

I landed on my face. I wore glasses at the time, and they shattered. In those days, optical lenses were made with regular glass, not the safety glass they use today. Splinters of glass pierced my eye and earned me a trip to the hospital. It took the doctor a few hours to remove all the glass from my eye. He told my mother that if one of the bigger shards of glass had gone one millimeter further, I could have been blinded in my left eye. That would have been much more life-changing than just having to wear special glasses for a month, which was what I had to do.

As I continued to grow, I got more competent at riding my big bicycle. A few years later, I found out there was a newspaper delivery route available. All I had to do was go down to a drop-off location where the bundles of papers were left, roll up the papers, fill my bike's baskets, and then ride around town throwing them into people's front yards. When I got good, I was able to take on a second route as well. I began delivering newspapers every day to about half of the town of Moab. I loved that job, and it allowed me to save some money. It was a good habit to get into, as I got used to doing something productive every day, even before breakfast and school.

Over the years, the laws changed, and kids were no longer allowed to do that kind of work. They could not be required to get up that early, but in my opinion, with extra sleep came a loss in learning good habits.

The Value of Hard Work

As a child, I found many other opportunities to make money. Besides my newspaper route, I would read my Bible (Grandma gave me twenty-five cents for each book of the Bible that I read), collect pop bottles, pull weeds, paint trim in the house, and do chores around the house (for which I was paid a weekly allowance). As a youth, I learned quickly about our family practices of tithing and saving. Although I rarely might spend some change on a candy bar, most of the time my income was saved.

In my early teens, I discovered a way to combine these financial options of tithing, saving, and spending into one practice. After our younger sister was born, my sister Shirley and I had the idea of giving our mom a mother's ring. This ring would have the birthstone for each of us four kids in it. We checked with the jeweler on Main Street, found out what the cost would be, and started saving. Fifty dollars was a lot of money to come up with, so we decided to save even more than our regular tithe—we saved 15 percent of everything we got. It took a while, but we achieved our goal and were able to buy the ring.

At that point, I learned the truth of the saying, "It's better to give than to receive." No memory of earning income during that time of my life is as vivid as the time we were able to give that gift. Our mom appreciated the ring as well.

I also learned that not all work is for pay—at least not for direct payment. When I was about eight years old, we moved into a new, split-level house with three levels, and my dad thought about how nice it would be to have another lower level beyond the lowest level of the house. Under the entry-level, there was a crawl space that was really of no use. Dad's idea was to excavate it deeply enough so we could have another useful space. For a farmer like him, there was always a way to get a project done.

He was able to dig a trench under the foundation, so we had exterior access to the crawl space. The trench was wide enough that my red wagon could go backward down the slope and under the house. Using a pick and a shovel, Dad would fill the wagon, and Shirley or I would pull it out into the backyard and dump the load. At our age, a wagon full of dirt was about as much as we could handle. Over the months, we made more than

1,100 trips up the ramp with loads of dirt, and we removed more than fifty tons of dirt from the basement.

Once the dirt and rocks were gone, Dad finished the new lower level with concrete and block, and we had a new, usable room. In addition to storage, we were able to race cars on a track and compete in ping-pong. Those fun times were great payments for the work we did—much more satisfying than any monetary compensation we might have received.

Planning for the Possibilities

I learned a lot when I was a boy. I learned even more when I raced hard, running away from my boyhood on my way to manhood. I have the bumps and bruises to prove it. But learning is not where the life lessons end. We have to apply what we learned. We have to test the ideas and see if they are true. We have to be responsible for what we are responsible for. I can say I have had more successes than failures in this area of life, but I was not ready to be unconscious for a week and out of work for many months.

I'm sure you've encountered significant challenges at one time or another during your life as well. When I think about the situations I've been through, they seem to fall into two categories. Some challenges are unforeseen and traumatic— auto crashes, a TBI, job loss, death of a spouse, or loss of other support—while others are long and drawn out— retirement, cancer, legal issues, and aging parents.

My bicycle crash falls into the first category. We were enjoying a normal day, doing normal activities, and suddenly, everything changed. What followed the crash is an example of the second type of category—years spent in court, trying to get our normal lives back. Having dealt with both of these kinds of challenges, looking back and reflecting has given me a good perspective on how we handled them, what we did well, what we did poorly, and what we can change for the future to prepare for possible new challenges.

My family and I were poorly prepared for the traumatic challenge that arrived with my crash. It quickly became evident as the challenges multiplied. While I was still in a coma, everything else in my life seemed to crash as well. Our family dog had to be put down, a friend broke his ankle on our trampoline, Elizabeth was in a car crash that totaled the car, and, to top it off, the stock market crashed. Although I managed the vehicles and our finances, I hadn't made sure Elizabeth had access to our accounts or knew our investment strategies, so she wasn't able to take any appropriate action to protect us from a financial crash. My brain injury meant we were powerless to protect ourselves financially for quite some time.

Although it's counterproductive to spend too much time focused on what bad things could happen at any time, it is good to ensure that adequate planning and communication have been done, so the trauma is not exponentially increased. It is prudent to be aware of all the financial details, how to access them, how to pay the bills, what the plans are, and who to go to for good advice.

Because traumatic events happen so quickly, there is no way to do detailed planning in preparation. However, long-term challenges can be better prepared for despite the variety of potential results. In our case, as we considered our options, the possibilities varied widely. One possibility was that we could win our case. If that happened, repayment of the damages would put us back into a high level of income, similar to where we were when I was an officer of a national company. Alternatively, we might lose our case, and we might have to pay for the government's legal costs, putting us into bankruptcy.

Although the bankruptcy possibility was much harder to deal with emotionally, the planning aspect was easier. While we were continuing in the court battle, our CPA advised us about the financial risk of winning without a plan. He described a client who won the lottery, and in only three years was destitute, without any money. This is not an isolated situation. An article in *USA Today* says, according to the Certified Financial Planner Board of Standards, "Nearly one-third of lottery winners go bankrupt within three to five years, which is more likely than the average American."[1] We did not want to follow that path, so we took his advice and put together a team to help us manage a possible win. That team included a CPA, a certified financial manager, and a trust lawyer. This team would direct us to help ensure that any damage payouts were secure for the long term.

Our team has been very effective. They have enabled us to live without the detailed focus we had for years when we needed to make sure every dollar went where it was budgeted to go. Several financial terms apply to every aspect of our lives, especially when challenges might occur. These terms are *budget, spend, save, give,* and *invest.* If your life challenges put you in a position where you might be short on time, you can use these tools to get the most from the time you have available. You should have a budget. You should plan where and how to spend your time. Depending on your lifestyle preferences, you can find ways to give of your time or invest it in good causes.

The point of this is to realize that, for any aspect of life where we have limitations, like money or time, good planning will ensure those resources are well used to our benefit, and that benefit is even greater when we are confronted with big challenges. We have to learn the balance between planning and trust —between doing our part and knowing when to step back and trust God will provide. We make our lists, set our goals, and work hard to create the life we envision, but at some point, we have to acknowledge we're not in control of everything. There's

---

1. Eric Lagatta, "Lotto Regret: Pitfalls of Powerball, Lottery Winners Serve as Cautionary Tales as Jackpots Swell," July 19, 2023, *USA Today,* https://www.usatoday.com/story/news/nation/2023/07/19/powerball-mega-millions-winners-instant-billionaire-regrets/70430571007/.

peace in knowing that, while we plan, God sees the bigger picture, orchestrating things in ways we can't always understand. That's the beauty of his providence; we take responsibility, but we don't carry the weight of the world alone. Sometimes, the best thing we can do is take the next right step, pray for guidance, and trust that, even when things don't go as planned, they're still going exactly as they should.

3

DOING MY BEST

What you get by achieving your goals is not as important
as what you become by achieving your goals.
-HENRY DAVID THOREAU

Back in the 1960s, one thing that was very different from today is the idea of competition. Competition was everywhere, just as it is these days, but it seemed to be more of a collective type of competition; there was a greater emphasis on teamwork, shared goals, and contributing to progress as a whole. Achievement was valued, but there was less pressure on individuals to constantly outdo one another.

In my case, from a very young age, I had always been taught to do my best no matter what I was doing. When my siblings and I were given chores to do, when we were done with the job, Mom would always ask, "Did you do your best?" or "Is that the best you can do?" When she asked these questions, it was not with a critical or sarcastic tone; she wanted our assurance that we had done our best at that time. The best that a third grader could do was not the same as the best that a high school graduate could do, but it was a fair inquiry to ask whether each of us had done *our* best.

Don't be afraid to give your best to what seemingly are small jobs. Every time you conquer one it makes you that much stronger. If you do little jobs well, the big ones will tend to take care of themselves.

-DALE CARNEGIE

When my parents married, they were in a pretty difficult financial situation. They worked hard to get out of it, and my mother never forgot that experience for the rest of her life. Although raising four kids did not allow her to work a regular job outside the home, she did what she could to bring additional income into the household by sewing and decorating cakes for others. As kids, my siblings and I observed firsthand what it meant to do your best. When my mom made a shirt or dress for someone and saw it was not her best, she would take the garment apart and remake it. So, I learned to do my best by the instructions and examples she and my dad set for us.

It's interesting how this lesson translated into another part of my life. When she heard that I was in the hospital with serious injuries after my bike crash, my sister Shirley, who lived in Africa at the time, took the first available flight to be there for me. Because the flights out of Africa were only available on a weekly basis, it took two weeks for her to get to the hospital. By that time, I had been moved from the ICU to the Rehab ward, but I was not saying anything more than, "Yep." Upon hearing she was at the hospital, I mumbled, "From Africa," which let the doctors know I had some real awareness and memory. While she was there, in addition to spending time at my bedside, Shirley also helped me with other therapies. One day, the therapist was working with me to count and grasp the basics. With Shirley's encouragement to keep striving to do my best, the very next day, I was quicker than the therapist in doing math problems—so much so that the therapist thought I was writing random numbers on the page.

Shirley also motivated me to do more extreme walking than

the medical staff thought was possible. One day, a nurse temporarily took over Shirley's role in directing my daily walking therapy. When Shirley came back and saw my progress, she asked the familiar question, "Is that really your best?" Hearing that question, I immediately demonstrated that I could do even more than what the nurses already thought was impressive.

Doing My Best at School

I learned to do my best at school too. During third grade, my teacher Mrs. Unger did a good job of making me a good reader. As usual, that summer the public library had a reading contest for kids. The contest was open to everyone, with competitions for each age group. In the hot summertime in Moab, there wasn't a lot for a nine-year-old kid to do other than read and swim in the public pool. Although I wasn't competitive, I had lots of time, and I liked to read. This combination enabled me to win the competition for third graders; I read more books than anyone else my age.

The trend of "doing my best" continued every year. Since I was younger than everyone in my class, as time went on, there were plenty of battles that I lost, especially physical ones. But I kept going, always striving to do a great job. Fortunately, when I was ready to start sixth grade, my mom got me into Ms. Madsen's class. It was a big deal because there were things she did differently than all of the other sixth-grade teachers. One of those things was teaching her students about the US Constitution. Her class was the only one in the entire school district that studied the Constitution in such detail.

Ms. Madsen turned this study into a competition as well. Her method was to give a trophy to the person who achieved the highest score on the test at the end of the Constitution study. She wanted everyone to strive to be the best in the class. However, she took it even a step further. Each year, she added another bonus question to the test, so, if a student got a perfect score, they could legitimately claim to have the highest score in history —to be the all-time best. Once again, my efforts paid off. I was able to get a perfect score, including answering all of the bonus questions correctly. I still have the trophy she gave me more than fifty years ago.

Over the years, although I was involved in plenty of physical activities at home, the area I excelled in was academics. In grades seven through nine (junior high), I began to have options as to which classes I took. Those options were typically based on how well I did in previous classes, so I ended up in the high-level classes for math, science, etc. The same group of kids were usually in the same classes, and we would often compare test scores, even though there was no defined or stiff competition. As I kept doing my best, one of my personal goals was to get a report card with straight As. Taking the advanced classes made it difficult, but it was still my goal even though I didn't achieve it in junior high.

During the spring semester of my junior year in high school, the challenges multiplied. Because I was younger than most of the other juniors, I had to wait until January to get my driver's license. Being able to drive opened the floodgates of life for me.

Kids are always looking for better transportation, whether it's advancing from crawling to walking or riding a tricycle to a bike. I had wanted a car since I became a teenager. It would have been nice to have a sporty model, but I thought anything to get me down the road would be great. One day, my dad told me one of his fellow workers was selling his car, which he drove fifty miles a day each way to and from the missile base. The good news was that he only wanted fifty dollars for it—and an additional thirty dollars for the radio. The bad news was that it consumed a quart of oil every day during his commute. The body was in good shape, though, and it was only about seven years old. Dad offered to help me fix the mechanical problems, so I agreed to the deal. The seller then changed the terms and said he wanted to sell the radio and the car together, so my cost went up to $80 for a '67 Mercury Comet Capri. I was probably not much help, but with another $300 in parts, Dad was able to rebuild the engine, and I was thrilled to have a working car on the road.

Now that I had transportation, I was able to get a real job working at a local grocery store. With a car and money, I also was able to date girls. What a change! A car, a job, girls—what a different life! In addition, I took a week off that semester to travel to Denver for a Basic Youth Conflicts seminar. My life no longer consisted of just focusing on my classes. Dealing with all of these new distractions made it tough for me to concentrate on getting good grades.

When I got to the end of the semester, I was pretty sure I had missed another opportunity to get straight As because I had been struggling in my drafting class. In that class, each assignment was scored individually, so by the end of the semester, I knew my score wouldn't qualify for an A. However, one of the other differences back in the '70s was that report cards were still completed by hand by each of our teachers.

Imagine my surprise, then, when I picked up my report card a week after school was out to find that Mr. Pierce had given me an A in drafting! That A matched all of my other grades on that report card. I was so excited to finally achieve my goal of straight As!

And then there was a family bonus. Many of the other kids in my school were rewarded by their parents for getting good grades. Some would get $1 or even $5 from their parents for every A on their report card. There were no such enticements in my family. We just were expected to do our best. Even though we had never been offered a prize for good grades, Mom and Dad came up with a new plan. If we got straight As, they would buy us a banana split at the local Tastee-Freeze. That first one was *sooo* delicious. I don't remember how many banana splits I was treated to after that, but that first one was not my last.

High school classes today are significantly more competitive compared to the 1970s. With an increased emphasis on college admissions, standardized testing, and extracurricular achievements, students often face heightened pressure to excel academically. Advanced Placement (AP) and International Baccalaureate (IB) programs are more widespread, requiring rigorous coursework that wasn't as prevalent in the '70s. Additionally, the growing use of technology and access to information has raised expectations for students. When I was in school, it was a more relaxed academic environment. There was less focus on college admissions metrics and fewer advanced course options. In that environment, academics were not seen as a competition, so students weren't aware of their class rank. If someone wanted to get good grades, they just had to take easy classes. There were no extra points for the higher-level classes, so for calculating your grade point average, an A in basic math was the same as an A in trigonometry or algebra 2.

One of the benefits of doing the best I could was that I never got sent to the principal's office in high school—at least not for any disciplinary measures. Since I had decided to apply to three military academies, the school administrators had to fill out a lot of paperwork to validate my applications. Because I was hoping to go to one of those schools, I didn't apply for any cash scholarships. When it came time for the high school to have the annual awards ceremony in a local auditorium, many of the seniors in my high-level classes were called forward to receive their awards. Apparently, someone pointed out that it was strange that my name wasn't being called since my academics were comparable to the other award winners. The school found an unusual way to resolve the inconsistency. They made up a new award just for me; they called it "The Most Paperwork Award" because they had to do so much more paperwork in triplicate to support my future educational goals!

Then, a week or so before graduation, I was called to the principal's office. Not just the administration office but the *principal's* office. I was very concerned, but I went directly to see Principal Thereon Johnson. When I got there, he said he needed me to do something right away, which added to my anxiety.

"Jimmy," he said, "I need you to go home right away and get a photo of yourself so we can publish your status as the class valedictorian in the local newspaper this week."

What good news! I didn't even know I was in the competition—and I had won! I guess I really did my best.

These stories might make it sound like I'm trying to make you believe that if you do your best, you will always win the competition. I would learn otherwise soon after my high school graduation.

About a week after graduation, I found out I was awarded my first choice in appointments to the military academies—the US Coast Guard Academy in New London, Connecticut. A few short weeks later, I was required to do my best among the more than 300 other cadets who had also achieved entrance to the most competitive secondary school in the United States. During my first couple of years, I learned so much. One of the most valuable lessons I learned was understanding the difference between *ability* and *effort*. Although virtually everyone was academically in the top 1 percent of their high school graduating class, I observed two different scenarios. One of my classmates studied harder than anyone else. He stayed up late every night studying, but he ended up failing and dropping out during our sophomore year. He wanted to be a coastguardsman so badly, but he was not able to meet the extreme, high-level academic requirements. Then, there was my roommate. His abilities exceeded anyone I have ever known. Despite double-majoring in engineering, and while participating in distracting extracurricular activities, he never really spent any time seriously studying. Despite his lack of effort, he still achieved honor-roll grades each semester. That was the difference between desire and ability. You had to have some of both and do your best with all that you had.

I believed I had adequate ability, and I was determined to give all of my efforts to achieve my best. I ended up right in the middle of my graduating class, which included only about half of those who entered the Academy with me. This theme has continued throughout my life. Some do better than I have done, and many do worse, but I just continue to do my best and leave the results up to God.

Adventures on the Bramble

In 1982, I was an officer on board the Coast Guard Cutter Bramble, a buoy tender, and that spring proved to be a difficult season. Despite being short-staffed, our commanding officer took on extra duties, and he worked the crew hard and long hours, for days, weeks, and months. Unfortunately, he did this without any recognition of the crew who worked under me. Having a baby at home and another baby due any day made for real challenges in my personal life, so I was basically in survival mode at work. As an example, even though I found coverage for my shifts, the captain would not allow me to go home to be with my wife when she was in labor, giving birth to our second child. My enlisted crew knew about the challenges, and they worked hard without complaints. Although we were a military organization with appropriate ranks, my crew did something very unusual when I was finally in the process of being transferred from the ship. Although they were enlisted, and I was an officer, they took me out to lunch as a goodbye. They also gave me a modified uniform item, reflective of my situation. Part of the routine uniform was a baseball cap with USCG Bramble stitched on the front of it. My crew modified a hat by adding "I

Survived" above the ship's name. This hat gave us all a good laugh.

With replacement officers assigned, the Bramble was now overstaffed. However, the captain required that I go on one more cruise. As we returned to port, he asked me to take the con (nautical term, meaning control) of the ship to bring it into port and dock it. Because I wanted to honor the performance of the men who worked so hard for me, I decided to wear the modified cap they had given me. Although the captain saw it, at that time he didn't acknowledge it at all, although the executive officer laughed at the irony.

My docking of the ship went so well that the engineers said I set a record for how quickly it was tied to the dock. I was glad to honor my crew, even though I believe it led to an inappropriate evaluation by the captain that probably caused the end of my Coast Guard career. This is an example of how "doing your best" may be different, depending on the context of the situation and who is evaluating your efforts.

I've learned many things from many people, most of it through conversations. I remember a time when I got together with Joe to talk about how hard life seems to be.

"Joe, how do you keep going, doing your best, even when it seems like everything is against you?"

"Well, I've had a lot of experience. It hasn't been easy, especially when I was young. My older brothers hated me. Maybe I deserved it, maybe not."

"What kept you from giving up or giving in to despair?"

"Good question. And my relationship with my brothers wasn't even the worst part. You know, we are reconciled now, which is probably why the pain of my childhood doesn't seem so bad. But what I still feel sometimes is that I once worked for a guy who took advantage of me, demoted me, and showed favoritism because I was a bit of an outsider to the family business."

"Yeah, seriously, why are some bosses just awful?"

"It's not that he was terrible; it was that he didn't trust me. And while I didn't deserve to be treated that way, I hadn't yet given him any reason to trust me. So, I worked as hard as I could. I listened well. I stayed late. And I showed respect to everyone in the company. Mostly—and this was the hardest part —I kept trying to trust God with my reputation."

"Oh, man, I know what you mean. My Coast Guard days were a bit of a mess sometimes."

"It happens to the best of us. And for me, in that job, the guy finally learned to trust me and put me in charge of the entire company, even above the family members. Here I have to laugh because my brothers hated me, disowned me, and threw me to the wolves. I had no family, but God gave me a new family, even before my brothers and I got back together. God's grace really is sufficient, even if we don't see it when we are stuck in a hole."

I so appreciate Joe. He's walked through some difficult circumstances that led to extraordinary outcomes. Like Joe, day after day, year after year, I keep doing my best with the energy God so generously gives me.

4

THE CRASH

We take the good days from God—why not also the bad days?

I was just about to turn fifty years old. Life was busy and full. I was active in my church and enjoyed leading a men's study group. After recording a video to promote the group's meeting, Steve Burford, one of the associate pastors, complimented me, saying, "Jim, it looks like you've lost weight." He was right—my diet and exercise efforts were paying off, and I had lost ten pounds. I was feeling great.

A week later, everything changed.

We had just returned from a family trip to Connecticut to visit relatives. While we were away, there was a severe thunderstorm in Colorado, and it caused quite a flood in the gully just north of our house. It was so strong that it overwhelmed the culvert under the utility road, completely washing away the road, and leaving a four-foot-wide and four-foot-deep gap. The culvert was still in approximately the same location, but now there was no road over it.

The rest of the summer was full of work, church activities, family gatherings, and outings with friends. Over Labor Day, we trailered our boat from Colorado to Lake Powell in Utah, about an eight-hour drive, where we met up with my dad. We spent the weekend at the lake fishing, swimming, and waterskiing. It was the perfect ending to a happy summer season.

When we got home from Utah, it was back to the normal routine. Wednesday evening, September 3, I had plenty to do. After unpacking, cleaning out the car, and taking care of some chores around the house, I realized I had enough time before dark to work on my fitness by going for a quick bike ride.

Elizabeth was watching TV in the family room with the kids. I told her I was going for a bike ride. Engrossed in whatever they were watching, she said a quick "OK." I left the house on my bicycle at about 7:30 p.m.

To make my exercise aerobic, I had set a routine for my bike rides that took about twenty minutes. Virtually any time I went for a ride for exercise, I followed the same loop. I would leave our neighborhood, ride south on Struthers Road for a mile or so, turn right onto Northgate for a couple hundred yards, and then turn right onto the utility road that paralleled the interstate highway. I'd ride north on the utility road for a mile or so to the point where it was close to Struthers Road, which I would take back to our neighborhood.

Although the utility road was not pristine, I felt very safe riding on it for a few reasons. First, because it went across government property (the Air Force Academy), I believed it was adequately patrolled and maintained. Second, where it entered the AFA property, there were signs prohibiting motorized vehicles, so I wasn't worried about getting hit by a car or motorcycle. Finally, although it was bumpy with cracks, the fact that I was riding a mountain bike meant there should be no significant hazards on the utility road.

My ride that evening was pretty typical. Going north on the utility road, I dealt with an uphill grade for the first stretch, but then I crested the hill and started a slight downhill section to the gully. The gully was probably about twenty feet deep, so it was a good idea to build up speed on the way down to get up the steep north side without difficulty. However, on my way into the gully, I was annoyed because someone had put a row of small stones across the utility road as it was going into the gully. I had to slow down to avoid the stones, but I was happy that I didn't have to totally stop.

Due to the steep slope going to the bottom of the gully, the pavement that would have bridged the stream wasn't visible until I was about ten feet from crossing the culvert. That short distance wasn't nearly far enough for me to stop my bike, even at my reduced speed. Because there was no ramp, there was no way for me to lift my front wheel enough to jump the four-foot gap at the bottom of the gully. Instead, my front wheel crashed into the north side of the chasm, pitching me forward to the pavement on the north side of the gully.

Have you ever had a moment so intense that time seemed to slow down to a crawl, just like you see in the movies? Have you ever woken up from a nightmare with your heart still racing, hoping you could forget the terror as quickly as possible? I'd had a few of those moments, but nothing like this. As my eyes closed and the pain faded away, I lost consciousness for what could have been the last time.

I wouldn't learn until much later that the impact of my fall broke my jaw on both sides along with three of my front teeth and my four back molars. It also rattled my brain, resulting in a severe traumatic brain injury (TBI). I would lay on the side of the road for the next fourteen hours. I've since learned that it was unusually cool that night, which was significant because typically with a severe TBI, the brain starts swelling, and any warmth exacerbates the swelling and damage. This swelling of the brain against the skull causes severe pressure, usually resulting in death. While the cool temps may have given me hypothermia, they also helped keep me alive.

Where Is Jim?

At about 8:00 p.m., Elizabeth's son Richard began to worry about me. "Has Jim returned?" he asked her. Elizabeth didn't know, so she went to look for me in the house and then went to see if my bike was in the garage. When she saw it wasn't there, she went to our neighbor's house to see if I might have stopped there. When they said no, she became worried. She immediately called the sheriff to report me missing. She also called other family members and our church friends to let them know I was missing. The message spread quickly; it went around the world, even reaching my sister in Cameroon, Africa.

When law enforcement showed up at our house, they asked many questions, and they verified that my body was not anywhere around the house, as if Elizabeth had called them after she had killed me. Then, they got a call to handle a domestic conflict somewhere else and left. Although Elizabeth and the kids wanted to go looking for me, law enforcement advised them not to leave the house. They were concerned that if someone had been targeting me and kidnapped me, they might be targeting the rest of the family as well. As hard as it was to stay in the house all night, they did. Friends from church began looking, but they did not have any real sense of where I might have been riding my bike.

The next morning, the sheriff and his deputies returned to begin their search. Usually, they wouldn't begin searching for a missing adult until forty-eight hours had passed, but since Elizabeth told them my wallet and car keys were still where I'd left them, they reconsidered. Elizabeth also told them I had never been gone for such a long period, especially not after dark. I'm grateful that, for whatever reason, they decided to begin their search when they did. I later learned Elizabeth felt very stressed, having them at our house was overwhelming to her, so they left and met just north of our neighborhood on Struthers Road to determine where to start searching for me. It was 9:00 a.m., a bright, sunny day. By that time, I had been lying there for almost fourteen hours with no cover or protection.

Jesse Kurtz, a local TV news anchor, lived in the neighborhood east of Struthers Road, across from where the search and rescue team was meeting to put together a search plan. On that particular morning, Jesse decided to go for a run—something he rarely did—rather than go to the gym to work out before driving to work. As he passed the emergency vehicles on his way to run on the utility road, he was aware that something was going on, but he didn't stop to investigate further. He headed south on the utility road, which quickly started down into the gully.

As he was running southbound on the road down the slope into the gully, he saw a pair of blue jeans. He quickly realized there was a body in the jeans! As he processed that information, he felt sick, thinking he had happened upon a murder victim. You can imagine the thoughts in his mind as he debated whether he should go back and tell the emergency people what he had seen. It seemed obvious that the body he saw was connected to the emergency vehicles and crew he'd seen. Nonetheless, even though he assumed they knew about the body, he decided to go back and ask them a "dumb" question.

The search team was astounded to learn that he had found me already, and they immediately began a recovery mission. When they realized I wasn't dead, they called in a helicopter to transport me to the hospital. Unfortunately, due to traffic conditions, the helicopter pilot wasn't able to land, so an ambulance transported me to Penrose St. Francis Hospital in Colorado Springs.

One of the doctors at the hospital told me later that, if I had remained there in the direct sunlight for even another half hour, I probably would have been dead due to the heat causing excess swelling of my brain. It amazes me how the details happened exactly as they did for me to survive. Had the search team not moved from our house to Struthers Road, Jesse Kurtz would not have seen them and would not have been able to inform them so quickly. Had Jesse followed his usual routine and gone to the gym, he never would have been there to discover me in the first place. I could have easily been lying in the sun for another half hour and been found dead.

Here I see God's provision and protection at work. I can't help but think there is a real spiritual battle going on here on earth. While my rescue took place in a miraculous way, at the same time, events were unfolding that seemed to be intended to keep me from living. For instance, when the police came to our house the night of the crash, they unexpectedly had to leave quickly to deal with an unrelated domestic disturbance. This distracted the emergency team from looking for me, delaying their efforts for several hours.

There was also poor communication by law enforcement. The local fire department had just procured an infrared device that was specifically useful for finding warm bodies at night. If the sheriff had called them, with a quick scan from the highway, they would likely have found me within minutes. That call did not happen.

Fear was also a factor. Richard knew the route I usually took for my bike ride, and he wanted to check out the utility road. However, because it was after dark, and because law enforcement didn't know if someone had been stalking me, they would not allow anyone in our family to leave the house since they might be attacked as well. Richard would likely have found me quickly, but he was not allowed to search.

———

Joe was no stranger to trauma either. During my conversations with him, he told me how his own family turned on him and was filled with such jealousy and hate that they decided to kill him. Then, when one of his brothers decided to try and save him, the enemy of our souls found another method to punish him instead. "But I've learned that even when things look the most hopeless," Joe told me, "God is able to work things out for a good outcome. It might take longer than you expect, but God always comes through."

I pray you'll never experience a horrific bike crash or a traumatic brain injury, but in this world, no one escapes without some adversity or tragedy. Joe helped me see that's where faith and trust come in. Faith means trusting in God's timing and promises, regardless of how difficult or delayed they may seem. When we trust God, we can see the bigger picture. Even when life takes unexpected or painful turns, God can take action to protect us. We can know God is always working for our ultimate good behind the scenes.

5

A NEW NORMAL

Even though on the outside it often looks like things are falling apart on us, on the inside, where God is making new life, not a day goes by without his unfolding grace.

As you look back over your life, have there been times or seasons when you can identify a particular theme? Maybe you didn't even recognize that theme as you were in those seasons, but when you look back, they often are very well-defined. This was the case for me regarding the year after my crash.

It is amazing to reflect on how something traumatic can happen very quickly—in a matter of a few seconds. But the diagnosis, or understanding of the results of that traumatic incident, can take a year or more to understand. And the actual healing may take years—in my case, it was an entire decade. It's comforting to realize that, when you're dealing with a painful situation, you're not going to know all the implications of it all at once. Those implications often may be revealed over a long period, a bit like removing layers from an onion. And, just like peeling an onion, dealing with each new layer may bring new tears.

What is a diagnosis? Webster defines it as "the art or act of identifying a disease from its signs and symptoms; investigation or analysis of the cause or nature of a condition, situation, or problem." A diagnosis is figuring out what's wrong or what's going on when there's a problem.

When it comes to a medical diagnosis, the doctor takes on the role of detective. He or she looks at your symptoms, reviews your medical history, asks questions, runs some tests, and then puts all the clues together to name the issue. A diagnosis is the official explanation of why you're feeling the way you are so the doctor can help you fix it or manage it.

Bad News or Opportunity?

In my experience, another aspect of a diagnosis depends on your perspective: Is it merely defining some bad news, or is it somehow providing you with a new opportunity?

I'm thankful my first diagnosis was incorrect after my crash. I was not dead; I was not the victim of a murder, as the jogger thought I was.

The initial medical diagnosis, although very serious, was easy to define, given my specific symptoms. Because I was unconscious for fourteen hours until I was found, the brain injuries determined by the MRI showed bleeding in more than fifty places, and because of the amount of memory loss I sustained (I couldn't remember anything from the previous week), my brain injury qualified as severe by every metric.

Pretty quickly, the medical team also determined my jaw was broken on both sides, and I was missing several teeth. In fact, they could see one of my front teeth when they x-rayed my lungs. Thankfully, they were able to remove the tooth without significant surgery, but I've often wondered if this is why I've had a chronic cough ever since my crash.

Because I had so many injuries, the doctors had to decide which ones to address first. They decided the most important thing was to try and keep me alive. That was a good thing, but one of the consequences of that decision was that my jaw healed out of alignment. One of the joints healed higher than the other, so my jaw was crooked, and my top and bottom teeth only touched on one side.

This didn't just affect my looks; a jaw that's out of alignment can cause a range of physical, functional, and even emotional issues. For instance:

- Pain and discomfort: I experienced pain not only in my jaw, but also in my face, neck, and shoulders. Chronic headaches and earaches were also common.
- Chewing problems: The misalignment made chewing difficult, putting an extra strain on my jaw muscles. Those missing teeth didn't help either!
- Tooth issues: Over time, misalignment can cause uneven wear on teeth, leading to chips, cracks, or sensitivity.
- Jaw clicking or locking: I noticed clicking, grinding, and popping when I opened or closed my mouth, and sometimes my jaw would even get stuck when I tried to open or close my mouth. This is known as TMJ, for temporomandibular joint syndrome.
- Difficulty speaking: Severe misalignment made speaking more challenging.
- Sleep problems: This affected the quality of my rest.
- Postural problems: My jaw alignment issues threw off the balance of my head and neck, potentially leading to poor posture and more body aches.
- Emotional stress: The chronic pain and discomfort took a toll on my mental well-being, leading to stress, anxiety, and frustration. The number of doctors' appointments alone was quite stressful.

During the first year after my accident, the medical team, with the help of my family, observed several symptoms and made medical diagnoses. I wasn't aware of many of them, and those I was aware of I didn't fully understand. These included:

- Lack of balance: Initially, I couldn't even walk alone, and sadly, I could no longer ride my bike. My lack of balance didn't only affect me; it changed our family's lifestyle. We had to sell the dirt bikes we enjoyed so much. The boat, the quads—they all had to go.
- Lack of hunger and appetite, and control of body temperature: This was diagnosed by me, and I brought it to the attention of my doctors.
- Lack of mental competency: I could no longer work as an executive, which of course resulted in a big reduction in financial resources. My boss Rob was the one who identified this as it related to my work in helping him build a new company.
- Very low brain-processing speed: Diagnosed by LearningRx—this was a beneficial diagnosis, as it led to being a part of their program with pretty incredible results (more on this in a later chapter).
- Lack of memory, both short-term and long-term: I couldn't remember previous projects I had worked on, and I could not remember many names or common words.
- Lack of motivation: I experienced regular bouts of depression on a weekly or sometimes more frequent basis. My dad diagnosed this one.
- Lack of adequate blood flow to parts of my brain: This was determined by a SPECT scan and was revealed during the testing required by lawyers preparing for trial. (A SPECT scan is a type of imaging test that uses a radioactive substance and a special camera to create 3D pictures of blood flow.)

- Broken pituitary, low testosterone, low growth
  hormone: These were diagnosed by an endocrinologist
  and confirmed by an MRI, but this took a year to
  figure out.

While I was grateful to have all of these various diagnoses, the dilemma I faced was that, for many of them, there were no known remedies. The doctors told me I should expect to improve mentally for about eighteen months, but then I would most likely reach a plateau, and after that, I shouldn't expect to improve further.

When I reached that plateau, I was not satisfied with my level of recovery. I had never been satisfied with less than doing my best, and I wasn't going to stop now. If I had come this far, why couldn't I expect to go farther? So, I did not stop pursuing other therapies. I was both patient and persistent. I knew I had a long road ahead of me, but I was determined to move past this plateau and continue to improve as much as I could. I was able to successfully apply some of the therapies I discovered as long as thirteen years later. I also wasn't afraid to be a guinea pig when it came to therapies that were still considered experimental . . .

This aspect of my situation reminds me of a story Joe told me one time after he was released from prison. As bad as that place was, as long as he consistently continued to be patient and persistent, he achieved things that no one else ever dreamed he would.

Hunger or Appetite?

As I mentioned, one of the symptoms I brought to the attention of my doctors was my lack of appetite. Over the years, while I was a corporate executive, I steadily added weight to my body.

Pound by pound, year after year, the additional weight became unhealthy and unsightly. Two behaviors contributed to this situation—eating too much and exercising too little. In my mind, when life gives you lemons, skip the lemonade and go for a waffle! Not exactly a low-calorie treat.

If you are like the majority of Americans today, you most likely are dealing with a similar situation, or you live with someone who is. The United States has been grappling with a growing obesity epidemic, with rates climbing steadily over the past few decades. This trend is fueled by a combination of factors, such as:

- widespread availability of high-calorie, processed foods
- sedentary lifestyles
- rising levels of stress
- insufficient sleep

And obesity affects more than just adults. According to the Centers for Disease Control and Prevention (CDC), more than 40 percent of adults and 20 percent of children are classified as obese. The prevalence of obesity is not just a matter of individual health—it has far-reaching implications for the healthcare system, creating a vicious cycle of poor health outcomes.

Before my accident, my strategy was to reduce my food intake and increase my movement, which I hoped would result in significant weight reduction. This may all seem pretty obvious, but this is another aspect where my story takes an unusual turn.

In my attempts to lose weight, it turned out that I was very successful—but not by the strategy I had planned. This part of my story is about *consumption*.

Obviously, I couldn't control my intake of nutrients while I was in a coma, but I was thankful the doctors and nurses were diligent about feeding me, even after I was awake. As a side note, during my time in the hospital, out of necessity, they were able to find new ways to feed me that left quite an impression on my body. Due to my neck damage, they were not able to insert a feeding tube down my throat. Instead, they cut my belly open so they could insert a tube directly into my stomach. Now, I have a six-inch scar and a dimple that is a reminder of a very creative way to eat.

After I left the hospital, though, I quickly found that I often didn't have any desire to eat. I began to consistently lose weight. I realized eating was an important thing to do, so I forced myself to do it at the standard appointed times—breakfast, lunch, and dinner. But I no longer bothered with the snacks that were previously part of my daily routine. I didn't give my lack of appetite much thought; I just assumed it was part of my new routine.

Christmastime that year brought home my eating challenges. Just a week or so before Christmas, Rob and Dianne, the owners of the company I had worked for before my accident, invited me to a company Christmas party at their house in Denver. By that time, I had recovered my ability to drive and had my driver's license again, so I was able to get there without any difficulties. The party was enjoyable, and I partook in the goodies, but not to excess. Because of my TBI, though, Rob didn't want me to risk driving home at night, so he asked me to spend the night at their place.

After a good night's sleep, I realized that, if I didn't wait around at their place for breakfast, I could make it back to Colorado Springs in time for church that morning. So, after saying goodbye to Rob and Dianne, I headed out, arriving just in time for the beginning of the service.

After church, the usual family activities consumed the afternoon. For whatever reason, I didn't have lunch that day, so I hadn't eaten since the night before. Late in the afternoon, I experienced a headache. I knew right away what caused it. Many times, earlier in my life, I had occasionally fasted for a day. Each time I did, the afternoon welcomed me with a headache, presumably caused by the low level of blood sugar in my body. When a headache hit me, I realized I had unintentionally been fasting that day.

But what immediately struck me was not that I had a headache—it was the fact that I hadn't experienced a single hunger pang during the entire day. In the past, before my crash, anytime I had fasted, I would start the day with hunger, and those hunger pangs would continue during the day before eventually resulting in a headache.

I had never realized how intricately our brain is connected to all aspects of our body's desires and behaviors. Although I enjoyed eating frequently before my TBI, now I didn't have an appetite, and as this day proved, I didn't have any hunger either.

My lack of desire for food continued for several more months. During that time, I continued to try and eat on a normal routine, but I also lost a total of fifty pounds. And then, for whatever reason, after about six months, I regained both my appetite and my hunger for food.

Loss of appetite can be helpful relative to weight control, but I do not recommend the TBI method of getting rid of this. And while I am very happy to have my appetite back, I now need to find other good ways to control it. And I make waffles for other people more than I eat them myself.

The Things We Take for Granted

During those six months without hunger, I also found there were other things our brains do that we never think about. For instance, during my routine walks to the grocery store, one day I noticed that, although I was not uncomfortable, I was the only one in the store wearing a jacket. This puzzled me. Why did I need a jacket to keep warm when those around me did not? As I thought about it, I realized there were also times when I did not feel the need to wear warm clothes despite the cool weather; I didn't feel chilly when other people did. The more I observed this, the more I realized that my body's temperature control wasn't working normally. I began making sure I dressed appropriately for the weather, no matter how it felt to me.

During these same walks to the store, I came to realize how quickly my mental capacity could be gone. During these walks, when I had almost reached the store, I had to cross a busy, four-lane road, complete with turn lanes. Often when I got to the intersection, I would check the oncoming traffic, but I couldn't ascertain whether it was safe or not to cross. Not knowing whether the next steps I needed to take would be safe or not was very frustrating. Since there was a McDonald's across the street from the grocery store, I often went there to sit for a few minutes until I could recover my senses. After a few minutes of rest, I was able to determine when crossing the road was safe.

Just as with my appetite, after several months, that aspect of my brain was healed, and I no longer had to deal with these deficits. Most people take these things for granted, but not me. I am grateful each time I experience hunger, each time I feel hot or cold, or each time I am able to walk confidently and safely across a street. Now, I can once again rely on my brain to direct my routine actions each minute of the day.

Giving Thanks

Michael Hyatt, author of *Your Best Year Ever*, says gratitude makes us resilient by keeping us hopeful.

> While our circumstances might be bad, they can also be better . . . Gratitude keeps us positive, optimistic, and able to keep coming back for more when life throws obstacles

in our way . . . Gratitude reminds us . . . we have the power to act and effect change in our lives.[1]

When you have hope, expressing thankfulness is a natural outcome. If you're anything like me, it's not always easy to be thankful, especially in the midst of hardship. It can be a difficult lesson to learn, as I can attest.

What has been difficult for you to learn in your life? Some people find it hard to learn math. For others, learning another language is a real challenge. One of my obstacles is learning names, especially remembering people's names when I first meet them.

During the process of going through everything I went through involving my crash, it is interesting what I learned about learning. One of the biggest learnings I encountered was how to be thankful. Going through an almost-fatal crash and suffering the resulting traumas may not sound like something to be thankful for, but that is what I learned.

Because my faith is important to me, I try to be consistent in reading the Bible. As soon as I was able, I got back into that routine during the months following my crash. Six months after my crash, I was reading the letter that another James (not me) wrote to the church throughout the world. I found it interesting that the first thing James mentions is going through various trials. That got my attention because I was going through trials of many kinds at that time. Since I was dealing with physical, medical, and financial trials all at the same time, I paid attention to James' instructions. His direction was for me to consider it all joyful during my time of trials.

Now, that was surely a dilemma. How could I consider all of this pain as *joyful*? As I reflected on this, I decided that, if I was supposed to be joyful, that meant I should first be thankful for

---

1. Michael Hyatt, *Your Best Year Ever: A 5-Step Plan for Achieving Your Most Important Goals* (Grand Rapids, MI: Baker Books, 2018), 91.

the situation. As I studied a little more, pretty quickly that understanding was confirmed when I read the conclusion of Paul's letters to Ephesus and Thessalonica; he said we should give thanks in *all* circumstances.

What else did James say about being joyful? He says to be joyful in the midst of trials and tribulations because we know what the results of those trials are going to be. You might think it would be easier to be joyful *after* we experience some positive results, but James says the joy must come first; the good results come later.

I decided to test this in my own life, and I found this strategy to be very true. After I began to give thanks for the situation I was dealing with, I began to see the benefits all around me. One outcome was that I was able to relate to and encourage others in their times of difficulty, and I was able to offer people suggestions on how to deal with medical issues. Over the years, the list of benefits of being thankful and joyful about my situation continues to grow.

I have often said that it took me six months to learn to be thankful, but in reality, it took me fifty years and six months—with my crash being the trigger that started my time of real learning and real experience of the power and joy that comes with giving thanks in all things.

I wanted to discuss this with Joe, so the next time we met, as we sat with our coffee, I broached the subject. "Joe," I said, "with all you've been through, how were you able to consistently thank God?"

"There's power in being thankful in all circumstances," Joe explained. "I've experienced both the highs and lows of life, but no matter what, I've consciously chosen to thank God and trust him."

I've learned to do the same. There are so many instances where I've been able to see how God has protected me and provided for me in unexpected ways. And of course, I believe he can do the same for you!

6

THE HEALING CHAIN

Every detail of our lives is worked into something good.

Regarding many aspects of life, I like using the analogy of a chain. It has many aspects that help me understand and describe different processes and results. Here are some key aspects of a chain that make it a useful comparative analogy:

- It is made up of multiple, defined links.
- Each link is well-defined and individual from all of the other links.
- The chain can be weak or strong, but only as strong as the weakest link.
- The chain can be short or long.
- What the chain connects and moves may not be known by each link, but if you pull on the chain, there will be a resulting action somewhere else.

The chains related to the healing I have experienced include these links[1]:

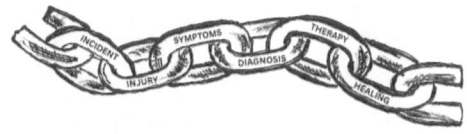

Here I will try to describe some of the healing chains I have experienced. Hopefully, you will see that even when the chain is not well-defined ahead of time, it is often worthwhile to pull on the chain anyway. It may end up helping resolve a situation.

For six years after my crash, I kept my eyes open for things to learn relating to my TBI. I knew the first couple of links in the chain—the incident was a crash; it resulted in a severe TBI, and it caused many symptoms. I hadn't understood those symptoms in any organized manner; however, since I was doing my best to learn and was always watching for opportunities, when I saw one, I grabbed it as quickly as possible.

One late summer evening, Elizabeth and I went out to dinner with our neighbors Eddie and Kynda. We occasionally enjoyed dining together, just as we did that evening at a nearby Mexican restaurant. The evening was pleasant, but the service was unusually slow. It was so slow that the waitress apologized to us three times, telling us she had no idea why the food was delayed so long. We didn't mind, though. We just enjoyed our conversation at the table and figured we wouldn't have to go anywhere else for dessert since we had so much time together at dinner.

Finally, after a nice meal, we strolled out to Eddie's car to ride home with them. The women got to the car ahead of Eddie and me, and while we were walking, an acquaintance of Eddie's was

---

1. Healing Chain graphic created by Alyzsa Crosby

just getting out of his car. When he saw Eddie, he stopped him to ask a quick business question about a potential golf tournament. Since it was Eddie's business, I stayed out of the conversation. However, I suddenly overheard him say he was looking to do fundraising for an experimental TBI therapy, and my ears perked up. They were looking for fifteen veterans who had suffered TBIs during the past several years. I quickly let him know I was qualified, and I asked if I could participate. Thankfully, the answer was yes!

The therapy they were testing was called Photobiomodulation (PBM), otherwise known as light therapy. Developed by Hungarian Endre Mester in 1967, this therapy had been approved and used for years to improve blood flow in the extremities (hands and feet) of diabetics. Exposing these parts of their bodies to near-infrared illumination on a regular basis improved their blood flow and prevented the need for many amputations. Someone realized the long-term symptoms TBI victims suffered were due to a lack of proper blood flow in their brains. Realizing how this therapy helped diabetics, they decided to try it out on the brains of TBI victims.

I estimate thousands of veterans are also TBI victims in Colorado Springs. I felt very blessed to be one of the fifteen chosen guinea pigs to be part of this experimental trial. Since it was a new usage for BPM, there was no device specifically designed for usage on the head, so the researchers had to make up a strategy to expose TBI patients to light therapy. Starting that October, for twenty minutes each time, I allowed the technicians to expose the top of my head to this illumination treatment three times a week. Each session made my head feel warm, but it wasn't uncomfortable or painful.

After six weeks, the doctors did another SPECT scan to see if the blood flow in my brain had improved. It had! Amazingly, it was back to normal. In addition, while I was going through this therapy, I realized that, after four weeks of treatment, I was no longer experiencing the weekly bouts of depression that had begun at the time of my crash.

Think of driving down an interstate highway where the speed limit is 65 mph. How well would you handle the traffic if your car had a top speed of 15 mph? No blood to the brain is like getting no gas to the engine—you just can't get up to speed.

There may have been other symptoms that the light therapy resolved, but I was especially thankful the depression was gone. Thinking back, when I jumped on the light therapy bandwagon, I had no idea what benefits to expect; I just knew they were trying to help me heal.

It was a very good gamble.

Brain Training

A couple of years after completing the light therapy, I happened upon another opportunity to be a guinea pig for TBI therapy. This opportunity began with another random connection. Ten years before, Elizabeth met a woman named Lisa at a computer class. Lisa was also from Connecticut, and they became friends. With all the changes that happened over those ten years, they hadn't kept in close contact, but they reconnected with each other when Lisa showed up at our church one Sunday.

After seeing Elizabeth in church a few weeks in a row, Lisa made an unusual connection. The company she worked for (LearningRx) was looking for six TBI victims who could be subjected to their brain training process while LearningRx documented all of the medical details of any changes in their brain function using Functional Magnetic Resonance Imaging (fMRI). Once again, I raised my hand, since I was interested in any opportunity to improve how my brain worked.

LearningRx was started in 2002 by Ken Gibson, an optometrist who had struggled with learning issues and saw that many of his patients also had difficulty with reading and other cognitive skills. He became passionate about researching ways to "train the brain" and give individuals the skills needed to think and learn. Today, LearningRx is considered the largest brain training company in the world, with brain training offered in more than 300 centers around the world.

This time, I went through a great deal of testing, so I had some idea about what benefits I might gain from their intervention. They did a resting fMRI of my brain, a qEEG, and an IQ test. There were also some tests to determine how good (or bad) my brain's processing speed was, how well my brain took in information from my eyes and ears, and how good my short- and long-term memory was. The most memorable test result was my brain's processing speed. Going back to the highway comparison, even though I had good blood flow in my brain, the best I could do on that 65-mph interstate was about 25 mph. I could not get up to speed or keep up with the regular traffic. So frustrating!

LearningRx took all of these results and put together a plan to exercise my brain. It was similar to working out at the gym with a good coach who directs you to lift the right weights, do the right number of reps, and get a little stronger each day. Once the testing was complete, LearningRx exercised my brain three times a week for three months. Then they repeated all the tests—with amazing results. Even after several years of doing the best I could to improve my intelligence, in just three months, LearningRx was able to raise my IQ by more than twenty points. Even better, my processing speed was high enough that I was staying with the slower traffic, probably going around 55 mph on that interstate. Incredibly, my fMRI showed that my resting brain was normal; it was no longer working hard just to keep me alive. It is hard to cheat on an MRI.

LearningRx was so pleased with the results that they decided to put me on a maintenance plan so they could see how I would do over a longer period. On this maintenance plan, I did the workouts once every two weeks for a year. At the end of the year, I was cruising with the traffic, right at the speed limit. They were so pleased with my progress that they even featured me in a short video.[2]

I've come to not only appreciate how LearningRx cared for me, but how they have a tremendous heart for people. They have gathered some inspiring and whimsical quotes and compiled them on their website. When you feel like you need a smile, go check them out.[3]

Here are two of my favorites:

- "Don't let what you cannot do interfere with what you can do." (John Wooden)
- "You're braver than you believe, stronger than you seem, and smarter than you think." (Christopher Robin, from Winnie the Pooh)

Do You Remember When?

Here's an oxymoron for you: Do you remember when you forgot something important? Since *forgetting* is defined as "a lack of a memory," how could you possibly remember you forgot something?

Well, I can affirm this oxymoron can be real, and I can give some frustrating examples of when I experienced that reality. My first memory of forgetting something happened during therapy, just a few months after my crash. The therapist was showing me simple ink sketches of common items, and my task was to let her know what those sketches showed. The sketches were of simple things—a table, chair, house, tree, and so on. As we were moving

---

2. You can watch the video here: https://vimeo.com/347180868/b0b50349a8.
3. https://www.learningrx.com/corp/blog/encouraging-quotes-for-students/.

through the pack of cards, we came to one that caused me to pause.

I was certain the expected correct response to this sketch would be "a flower." However, I knew it showed a flower, but I also recognized the specific flower in detail. I knew it was white and purple, I knew it grew in the mountains, and I even knew it was the state flower of Colorado. But I could not say its name. My frustration did not last long, as the therapist reminded me that it was a columbine. Since then, thankfully, that word has been reconnected in my mind to the visual of that flower. Now I can say columbine when I see one of these beautiful flowers. This was my first memory of something I forgot.

There were many other instances when I couldn't speak a word, even though I knew all the details, definitions, and usages of that word. Another specific example was when I wanted to contact a friend to get some of his famous barbeque sauce. Since I had worked with him at two different jobs for several years, I knew him well. In one of the jobs, he was based in Atlanta and managed a whole region of the company's buildings, so we communicated frequently.

My frustration started when I tried to remember his name. For an entire week, I used every research strategy I could think of to find his name, with no results. When I expressed how frustrated I was to my wife Elizabeth, she said; "Well, it could not have been Trey Terry, because he was based in Rhode Island." Although she remembered the wrong location, the link to that name was restored. I had Trey's name reconnected in my brain, so I could contact him and get some of the very good BBQ sauce he was known for.

Although I don't know all of the technical differentiators between short- and long- term memory, I had losses in both categories. Long-term memory includes words, names, projects I did at work, etc. For most of those, I had no idea that I had forgotten them, so I didn't realize my loss.

Once I finally started working as a maintenance guy at the

library, I realized what it meant to lose my short-term memory. It can cause havoc in your day. For instance, while I was working one morning, one of the librarians, Susan, showed me a light bulb that was burned out and needed to be changed. Early in the afternoon, someone asked me if I had seen Susan that day, and I said no. I had no recollection of my conversation with her. After this happened a few times, I started keeping a notepad in my shirt pocket where I could write reminders about things I needed to remember. Often, I would look at the pad, see something I wrote, and go take care of it, even though I did not remember writing the note.

A couple of weeks after starting my maintenance job, I visited a psychologist who my lawyer was using to test my brain. He quickly confirmed I was experiencing short-term memory loss. His findings were very detailed, and they gave my lawyers accurate information about the extent of my brain damage and the limits of my mental capabilities, which were dramatically reduced. Thankfully, he also was able to recommend Aricept, a medication that would help overcome the short-term memory failure I was experiencing. Although it is usually prescribed for Alzheimer's patients, he knew it also had helped many TBI victims with their short-term memory losses. And in my case, the medication was very effective.

Once I started on the medication, my memory improved. I didn't have to rely quite so heavily on my pocket notepad to get through the day successfully. It may not have been the best, but it got me through the day. But as you know, good things often come with bad things. Such was the case with this medication.

One of the common side effects was drowsiness; therefore, the doctor recommended I take my daily dose in the evening before bed. That way, the sleepiness side effect wouldn't be a problem; it would be a benefit. But shortly after I started taking it at night, I found out the hard way about another, rarer side effect—extremely vivid dreams. For example, one night Elizabeth found me climbing over her in bed, as I was trying to protect her from an attacking villain in my dream. The dreams were so vivid that, when I woke up in the morning, I would think I needed to fix the problem with the car I remembered finding out about the night before.

This was a new dilemma. I liked having a good memory, but I also liked having a safe wife. Fortunately, my engineering mind took over and resolved to solve the problem. I figured that the intense dreams I was having were due to the high concentration of the medication in my body. Based on my reasoning, I thought if I took the daily dose in the middle of the day, its level in my body would be low enough by bedtime that I would not have those rare side effects. Thankfully, that strategy worked, and I was able to take the medication for several years without any more negative side effects.

Speaking of vivid dreams, my buddy Joe has the ability to not only dream in great detail but also interpret what his strange dreams mean. As a young boy, he had dreams about his brothers' sheaves of grain bowing to him. He also saw the sun, moon, and stars bowing to him. When he shared these dreams with his brothers, they were irritated and annoyed with him, but later in life, his ability to interpret dreams was part of a larger plan to save his family. Things don't always make sense, but Joe and I have had many conversations about trusting God for wisdom no matter what. Even in adversity, God can orchestrate events in strange and unforeseen ways. We often can't see a way through our challenges, but our part is to trust and take the next step. As I can attest, the results can surprise you!

How good is your memory today? Through the years, doctors and therapists repeatedly asked me that question, so I found an easy way to test my short-term memory and see if it was improving or declining. Often, it is my turn to go to the grocery store to pick up a few items. It doesn't matter whether I am walking the mile to the store or driving. I found that if I make a list of the items I need to get, it's easy for me to remember how many items were on the list. For example, one Wednesday there were six items to purchase at the store. Now, if I wasn't confident in my memory, I would write the list and put it in my pocket. When I got to the store, I picked up everything I remembered from the list, relying on the number of items I had found to determine if I remembered everything. If I was one or two items short, then it was time to exercise my memory to find what was missing.

Over the years, this has been a good method to exercise and check my memory's effectiveness. These days, I can usually remember the handful of items and get them without looking at the list.

One of the other results of this therapy was a benefit I had not anticipated. After my crash, I lost my job because I didn't have the mental capability to do that level of work any longer. However, after the healing I experienced through the Learn-ingRx therapy, I called my former boss Rob to tell him I had gotten my brain back. He recognized the reality of what that meant, and he immediately hired me back into his company.

Over the years, these experiences have proved to be invalu-able. Occasionally, I have felt like my thoughts were not quite as quick as normal, so I've gone back to LearningRx for a quick assessment. When the tests showed some declination, I signed up for more maintenance therapy. That improved my brain processing enough that I was able to get back in the fast lane.

When I think about how these random connections resulted in such great benefit to me, it reminds me of Joe's story of random events. For instance, when he was able to give someone advice in an unusual situation, that person forgot about him but years later connected him to an amazing opportunity that led to a promotion where he went from a low-level manager to the vice president. God's providence is truly always at work on our behalf!

As part of their process, the LearningRx testing confirmed that my short-term memory was one part of my brain's function that still needed improvement, even with the continued help given by the medication. Comparing my short-term memory to traffic flow on the highway where the speed limit is 65, I was moving with the traffic at just about the speed limit. But I was not going as fast as I had been accustomed to before my crash. Also, I was going this speed with a turbocharger running all the time. I would rather go faster without the continuous help.

After three months of cognitive training, LearningRx determined that my short-term memory was back where I wanted it to be. I wondered if it was because of the recent therapy or if I still needed medication to keep running well all the time. With that question, we ran a test. After a new short-term memory test, I stopped taking the medication each day. After six weeks we retested and found that my short-term memory was still just as good without the turbocharger. I did not have to worry about the potential side effects anymore, and my memory could cruise down the highway at a very good speed.

Down the Rabbit Trail

I've never spent much time analyzing myself. If I knew I did the best I could, that was generally enough for me. But during the years after my crash, I learned some new things about some of my abilities and even more about the abilities I lost.

After my crash, when I learned I wasn't able to go back to my previous job, my boss Rob described some of the characteristics he observed in me. He told me why they were important, and why the change made such a difference to him. The best way to describe the ability I had before my crash and lost afterward is the term *rabbit trails*. This term originally was used to describe the way rabbits and other small animals create winding, complicated paths in fields or forests. Today, the term rabbit trail typically refers to a person straying from the main topic or goal and going off on tangents. It conveys the sense of someone wandering off course in the middle of a conversation, project, or thought process. The key is knowing when to follow them and when to return to the original path.

Before my accident, Rob had been impressed by my ability to handle mental rabbit trails. When I had a defined project I was working on, I was effective at staying focused on that goal until it was complete. As with most jobs, often other small issues would arise during my completion of the project. Each time, I would quickly handle that rabbit trail and get back on track to continue toward the completion of the project. Rob's observation was that after my crash when I went off on a rabbit trail, I never got back on the original track. As a high-level manager helping build a national consulting company, this is a huge detriment—and it meant I could no longer perform my role.

While it was interesting for me to learn about the mental damage that had been caused, I didn't have any idea about what to do to rectify the issue. A memorable example describes the challenge this presented me with daily. While working at the library, since I was the supervisor and had many years of working with HVAC control systems, monitoring the control of those systems was part of my job. Whenever there was a challenge with how the air-conditioning or heating systems were being controlled, it was my job to investigate the system to determine the cause of the problem and then correct it by changing the programming. Not only were these very old systems, but the computer program used to run them was unfamiliar to me, so dealing with this kind of issue became a real challenge. However, I was thankful for the challenge, as I was always looking for new opportunities to sharpen my mind and exercise my mental skills.

One day, while I was working on resolving an HVAC controls issue in the computer programming, I dug deeply into the system and had just gotten to the point where I could focus on resolving the problem. At that moment, Robin, one of my techs at the library, walked in and asked me a question. Although his question was a simple one and required virtually no thought to answer, my mind saw it as a small rabbit trail. I lost my mental view of the big picture, and I had to start over from the beginning. It was very frustrating.

Today, after so much healing in my brain, I still understand the temptation to give in to rabbit trails, but I'm thankful they no longer keep me from completing whatever project or conversation I'm engaged in.

I like the smell of coffee. I like coffee shops even more. I love enjoying conversations with friends while sitting in comfy chairs, feeling the buzz of a local café. And I'm particularly fond of my times with Joe, listening to his story and learning about him and his faith. From him, I've learned that in God's economy, the weaker I am, the stronger I become. This is a real paradox, but Joe has helped me to see that God's grace is enough; his strength is perfected in my weakness. While I'd never wish an accident like the one I've experienced on anyone, I am grateful for the lessons I've learned through it. My injury began a chain of events that has resulted in one healing after another. My limitations have given me many opportunities to trust God and have faith that new doors will open and healing is possible.

7

ON THE JOB

Do your best. Work from your heart.

I've long been a fan of R.G. LeTourneau. I admire him as someone who never wallowed in his circumstances when they seemed unfair. When America entered World War I, a prior injury kept LeTourneau from military service. That was a big disappointment to him, so he found another way to serve. He left the auto garage he co-owned and served his country by working in a shipyard. His reward for that altruism? He returned to a bankrupt business that saddled him with serious debt. Unfair? Certainly. But never mind that. Mr. LeTourneau found work using his mechanical skills to repair a heavy-duty land scraper. The machine's owner asked him to level a forty-acre plot, and in the process, LeTourneau fell into a lifelong passion for the earthmoving business. The lesson: "Unfair" may be the open door you didn't know you wanted.

The film *Apollo 13* popularized the phrase "Failure is not an option," but R.G. LeTourneau lived that phrase long before. LeTourneau lived the belief that "problems are only opportunities in work clothes," as American industrialist Henry J. Kaiser once said. Finding his passion in earthmoving didn't prevent

LeTourneau from experiencing the potholes. Twice, he almost went bankrupt in that competitive niche of the construction business. But in facing those setbacks, he turned his eye not to moving earth but to the equipment that does it. He became an innovator, inventor, and industrialist. The young man "unfit" for World War I manufactured 70 percent of the heavy machinery used by the United States to win World War II. The lesson: Early failure leads to later opportunity. I would see this lesson play out in my career many times.

Choices, Choices

When it's time to make significant choices in our lives, we often talk about which open door we should choose to go through. However, as I look back at a lifetime of such decisions, I find that it doesn't work to use open doors as a way to describe the decision-making process I have followed. The choices in front of me often were not as well defined or separated as open doors are. In my experience, a more appropriate analogy related to making significant decisions like choosing which exit ramp to take while driving on an interstate highway.

Consider this: When you're driving down the highway, the significant decisions you need to make typically involve which exit to take, or whether to stay on a particular road longer. I hope this analogy will bring to mind the situations you encounter and help you make the best decision (i.e., take the right exits) to get you where you want to go.

Not surprisingly, I apply my philosophy of "doing my best" in this analogy. Taking an interstate highway usually gets you to your destination more quickly than taking the back roads, but if you take the highway, you'll have to go some miles down the road before you can change direction.

One of the first significant decisions in my adult life was the choice of education. I was on the highway for an engineering degree, and I wanted to get the very best engineering education at a reasonable cost. When a brochure opened my eyes to the possibilities that a military academy education offered, I decided it would be a good road to travel. The financial cost made it the best possible option, and the quality of the education was high.

If I drove west on one highway, I'd pass a sign saying the next three exits would take me to military possibilities. Other colleges were available down the road if I chose not to take those exits or if they were closed for construction. Thankfully, the nautical off-ramp was open, so I took it. It turned out that this led to a frontage road to the Naval Academy and the Coast Guard Academy. Since the Coast Guard road was my first choice but was quite congested, I kept both options open. Providentially, the traffic thinned out, and I was able to take the Coast Guard exit. That's how I ended up in New London, Connecticut, a month after graduating high school.

The Coast Guard provided me with a good education as well as good experience. Jobs were hard to find back then, so I was grateful to be given a job in the Coast Guard automatically. My time in the Coast Guard put me on a new highway of providing for my family. After several years, a new (life) traffic decision was approaching. I knew that any of the next three exits would take me where I wanted to go and adequately provide for my growing family. If I was able to stay in the Coast Guard, that would be a good career. If not, the engineering education I received there could enable me to find work as a design engineer or a facility operations manager.

Part of choosing a direction involves preparations. The better prepared you are for the possible routes, and the better familiar you are with the various exits, the more options you will have, and you'll be able to travel faster on the next highway. Although it was not required by the Coast Guard, and not useful for an operations position, I decided to pursue a professional engineering certification to improve my qualifications as a design engineer. That certification turned out to be helpful, even outside the design field.

Although I hoped to be able to have a long-term career in the Coast Guard, that turned out to not be an option. Eventually, this led me to the facilities management industry and a job managing the corporate headquarters buildings for GE Capital. I was grateful for God's provision, but due to corporate changes, after several years, I once again had to explore new career choices.

During that time, I was also planning to start a new business in the entertainment industry, although I continued interviewing for possible facilities management jobs. As I carefully considered how long our available finances would support us, I set a deadline to come up with the funds to start the new business. I was almost there, too, but then my fundraising plans failed at the last minute. That was disappointing, but I was able to quickly take the on-ramp back onto the facilities management highway, and I began working for Johnson Controls. Once again, God provided for me.

I had some great experiences working at Johnson Controls in new areas; I explored sales, schools, pharmaceuticals, and retail businesses. Sometimes one highway turns into another without any real change other than the highway number. That was the case for me, as my job suddenly ended at Johnson Controls, and I was hired by my customer United Rentals. I just kept doing the next right thing, trusting God was still providing for me. While at United Rentals, I went through some significant family changes—and then United Rentals went through something significant too. They went through a reorganization and, in the process, they abruptly removed my position—right after I had made the cross-country move from Connecticut to Colorado.

But the thread of God's provision and protection continued. We were in the process of building a new home in Colorado, and, thankfully, on the day our homebuilder required proof of income, I received two good job offers. That gave a new dilemma. Did I want to work for the well-known company

Coors, or did I want to take a job at the headquarters of an otherwise unknown company, AIMCO? Even though it potentially would require some travel, the AIMCO job was a shorter commute, so I chose it to have more time with my family. It turned out to be an important decision because that job turned out to be a big promotion, and I became vice president of a national company.

Twists and Turns

Sometimes the twists and turns in the road put us into unexpected situations. It's like a sign I saw on a highway many years ago that said, "No services available for the next 110 miles." It could be a long wait if you run out of fuel or need to make a pit stop during those 110 miles.

Just like that lonely stretch of highway, after my crash and resulting brain damage, the road ahead of me appeared very long, with no obvious places to fuel up. I wasn't looking for convenient exits along the way but for possibilities of provision to move me down the road. Many people facing this situation would take the last exit before that 110-mile stretch—the one marked Disability, and they'd take whatever handouts were available. That was certainly a temptation, but I made a different choice. I was determined to do the best I could along the way. After a year and a half, the best I could do was a maintenance job at the library. It didn't pay much, and it was far removed from being a vice president of a national company, but I was able to do the work, and it provided just enough income to almost keep us afloat financially.

At the same time, my eyes were opened to other possibilities. For instance, there was a possibility that someone was liable for what caused my bike accident, so we found a lawyer to help us pursue that option.

While I was grateful God had provided a maintenance job at the library, it was a time of concern for me and my wife. What would the future bring? Would it be a continuous, never-ending job that let us barely scrape by? Would we win a legal battle? Would my investment in foreign currencies eventually pay off? For me, the important thing was not to focus on any one of those possibilities but instead to pursue each of them the best way I could.

I'm grateful to say that, after eleven years, we won the legal battle. We were able to return to the lifestyle we lived before my crash. In the future, I know there will be another round of decisions to make, but I feel blessed that, in every situation, there's always more than one exit ramp to take.

Being without a job is no fun, even if you have a good excuse like I did after my bike crash. I don't recommend unemployment because you don't have much to do. If you want to do something entertaining or productive, it usually costs money, but you don't have that option because of your lack of income. You also have much more limited contact with other people, so it is easy to get depressed. Depression is a common symptom of a TBI, so, in my case, being unemployed made depression much easier to come by.

Before my bike accident, I was successful in quickly finding work when one job ended. However, after my TBI, that did not happen. Once I was back home from the hospital and feeling better, I followed the typical job-hunting processes: I signed up with the local employment center, attended job fairs, networked with contacts, applied for advertised jobs, etc. Occasionally I would get an interview, but they never were successful; they never resulted in a job offer. I had never dealt with this before, and my depression mounted.

This time of inactivity and frustration could have continued for years. In the course of my networking, I met many other victims of TBIs who had been dealing with the same symptoms and challenges for a long time. There are good reasons for this.

Those with TBIs can suffer from cognitive challenges, physical limitations, emotional and behavioral changes, and self-esteem issues. All of these things might show up during the interviewing process and paint the TBI applicant in an unfavorable light.

Divine Providence Intervenes

God had other plans for me. Looking back, it's amazing how several random pieces came together in my favor.

A little more than a year after my crash, I finally was able to do some real job hunting. Because of my TBI, I needed to look for different kinds of jobs than I had done in the past. I had to come to terms with the fact that I was not going to be a director or executive of a significant company, and I decided I would take whatever I could get.

I applied for a maintenance job with the Pikes Peak Library District (PPLD). I also applied for a job with USAA, a major insurance company. I had been one of their customers for almost thirty years. USAA was quick to respond to my application and hired me, so I was scheduled to start working for them after just a few weeks. But then, surprisingly, the day before I started working at USAA, PPLD called me and asked if I could interview for a job with them.

This was a dilemma. I knew I would rather do maintenance work for the library because it was better related to my previous career in facilities management, but how could I take time off on my second day on a new job to go for another job interview? Thankfully, PPLD was flexible and rescheduled my interview time for a Wednesday evening, after my working hours at USAA. The interview went well, but I encountered a new challenge—the amount of time it takes for PPLD to run a complete background check. Another waiting game!

The first few weeks at the USAA job consisted of training to enable me to get state certification in certain aspects of the insurance business. Internally at USAA, they have a competition to see if each class can have more people achieve certification than other classes in the past. On Thursday of the third week of training at USAA, I was scheduled to go to the state testing office to test for my insurance certification. Since the test was scheduled for noon, I arrived early and planned to eat my sack lunch in the car before going in for testing.

While I was eating my lunch, I got a big surprise. PPLD called and officially offered me the job! But despite the assurance I had the job I preferred, I felt the right thing to do would be to take the insurance test anyway. I did—and passed.

When I returned to USAA that afternoon and let them know I passed, they were thrilled because our class had set a new record for how many passed the exam. However, they were very surprised when I immediately resigned on the spot. Usually, people only resign after the test when they fail. They accepted my resignation with good wishes, and I started working at PPLD the following Monday morning. I was very thankful to be employed, and I was equally thankful that my depression had lifted.

Hope Shows Up in Unexpected Ways

We all encounter difficult times in life—times when the problems seem to pile on top of us like a whole football team on top of a fumble. A medical issue can turn into a financial crisis, and financial troubles often lead to relational challenges quickly. So, what do you do when life throws you a curve ball? How do you deal with life on a day-to-day basis? Where do you find hope?

During the summer of 2014, although we had won our case in court, it wasn't over. The other side was appealing the ruling.

Who knew what this court would decide or how long it might take? My wife and I had been dealing with inadequate finances for six years. How much longer would it be—and that's if the appeal possibly went in our favor? It was easy for us to focus on the hopelessness of our situation.

Although I knew we had good lawyers, I couldn't pin all of my hopes on them. I had to continue to be open to other possibilities that might come along. I was about to discover some exciting lessons about hope.

I was still at the library, maintaining the facilities. I had hired a new employee, the son of a friend, and he seemed to be a good fit for the job. But then, after only a month on the job, he left. This left me understaffed again, and I had to start over with the time-consuming, tedious governmental process of finding another maintenance worker. While it wasn't a high-level position, it was an important job to keep things running smoothly. I quickly learned that you never know what unexpected blessings might come with a maintenance guy like Randy, my new hire.

I had learned that the library liked to display people's unusual collections. For about twenty-five years, I have been developing a collection of more than thirty different paper currencies from around the world. These currencies do a great job of showcasing the differences of people, languages, and cultures. Some of them I had collected myself in my military travels, and others were obtained by friends, associates, or fellow workers. Since the library was interested, I brought my collection to work to display to the public.

Ironically, when I showed my collection to the maintenance guys, Randy shared with me the significance of a couple of them. They were currencies from countries where wartime had caused them to be devalued. One of them was the Iraqi dinar. In 2000, one dinar of that currency was exchanged for over $1. After the devaluation in 2003, a dinar was worth less than one cent. Randy told me that this and a couple of other currencies could potentially be revalued at any time, possibly back to their value before

Saddam Hussein's rule. It seemed to be a very enticing invest-ment, so over the next few years, I invested any birthday money I received in these currencies. During that time of economic hardship, it gave me financial hope. When I hired Randy, I never expected to get this in the package, but I was very thankful for it. Although the dinar has not yet been revalued, the hope it gave me was very encouraging, and it will be a pleasant surprise when it happens.

My conclusion is to not let difficulties keep me from living a full life during hard times. As Robert Schuler once said, "Tough times don't last; tough people do." When hard times hit, we should always keep our eyes open to unexpected sources of hope. A proverb I love says this: "Unrelenting disappointment leaves you heartsick, but a sudden good break can turn life around."

8

MY DAY IN COURT

Consider it a gift, friends, when tests and challenges come
at you from all sides. You know that under pressure,
your faith life is forced into the open and shows its true colors.

W hen we see someone get hurt, two questions usually immediately come to mind:

- How badly is the person hurt?
- Who is really at fault?

Sometimes we try to simplify matters. For instance, in my case, someone might say, "Oh, he suffered a severe TBI," thinking it completely summarizes the injury I experienced. However, for myself and the many others who have lived through such an injury, I can attest that there are many details we don't even realize ourselves—sometimes for years.

Likewise, it often is easy to presume to know who is at fault for a painful situation, but the reality often is never known this side of eternity. That being the case, we can spend tremendous amounts of time trying to determine who was at fault and to what degree they should be responsible for the damages they caused.

A commonly used phrase that is meant to question the fairness of any resolution regarding difficult matters in life is, "Did you get your day in court?" Often, this just questions the fairness of your outcome as opposed to implying you spent any time in a courtroom. Since more than 95 percent of people with situations that are serious enough to be filed in court are resolved without spending any time in the courtroom, most people get their day in court without going through all of the potential idiosyncrasies that are possible.

However, my day in court ended up taking almost fifteen years. It required spending actual time in the courtroom on six occasions, and it involved the court system up to the US Supreme Court.

After my crash, my boss Rob took action quickly. Based on the details of the situation, it seemed clear that someone might be at fault for the washout of the road crossing the gully where my crash happened. Since my wife wanted to make sure they were found and held to account, Rob offered to help her find a lawyer to pursue the case. He knew of a few lawyers he felt comfortable recommending, so while I was still in a coma, unable to help myself, he and Elizabeth started interviewing prospects.

The first interview was with David Hersh, a lead attorney with Burg Simpson, a national law firm with an office in Denver. It was not a one-way interview. Since it would be a contingent case, the attorney needed to be sure our case had merit and that we would see it through to the end. While Elizabeth was determining whether she could work with David, he was assessing whether we would stick with the case, no matter how difficult it became. At the end of their meeting, Elizabeth said, "This is who we want to represent us."

Rob protested because David was the first attorney interviewed, and he had additional lawyers lined up. However, Elizabeth was adamant, so those meetings were canceled, and an agreement was signed with Burg Simpson. Who could have imagined that the relationship would last for almost fifteen years before all of the legal action was completed? Considering this early part of our case, my advice is to make sure you choose your advisors well, ensuring they are someone you can trust fully to tell you both the good and bad news and who will have your best interests at heart. Elizabeth's intuition was right. David Hersh was fully qualified on all counts for us.

Who Is Responsible?

Sometimes it's clear who is at fault, so you pursue them for repayment of damages or other reconciliation. This was not the case in my situation. Since my crash happened on a utility road, which was washed out where it crossed a gully adjacent to a highway, it was not clear who was responsibility for the damaged road. Quickly, David and his team of attorneys realized the possibilities included:

- Colorado State Department of Transportation
- El Paso County
- One of the utilities that used the easements along the highway
- The designer of the wash crossing
- The company that installed it
- Whoever maintained the utility road
- The Air Force Academy, who owned the property

David determined there were possibly as many as twenty different entities to pursue in our case. Of these various entities, some had legal requirements that the case be made within as little as six months. Others had legal limits on liability, as low as

$500,000. If either of those were the appropriate entities, our case would have to be fast and cheap, so we would end up with some real reimbursement, not just the payment of legal costs.

It was a challenge to determine who had originally built the utility road and when. Part of the process involved researching old photos to determine how long the road had been there, so we could make an educated guess about why it was built and by whom. Pretty quickly, most of the various entities fell by the wayside as not being potentially liable—except the US Air Force Academy. If the pursuit of damages resulted in a lawsuit, the law required that it be filed within two years of the date of the incident that caused the damages.

In my situation, this was good news, considering that it took pretty much the entire two years to understand and quantify all of the medical damages I suffered. Suffice it to say that, during those two years, I saw many doctors and endured many different kinds of medical and mental testing procedures. The big pieces of damage included hospitalization, loss of income, loss of personal abilities, many therapies, lifelong medications, and so on. It was a grueling process, to say the least.

One Simple Question

Each of us can come up with examples when different witnesses of the same event tell dramatically different stories. Since our day in court had many limitations, and we wanted to ensure we would achieve a fair outcome, we needed to limit who we allowed the judge or jury to listen to. To do so, and to avoid wasting the court's time, one of the first steps in the legal process involved selecting witnesses through depositions. If a potential witness didn't have anything significant to tell, we weren't going to waste the court's time by calling them as a witness. The witnesses we chose included family members, friends, and doctors. At times, we also had to listen to people that the other side chose.

The depositions don't take place in the courtroom; they provide a chance to hear someone's story under oath in preparation for court. This might be compared to a professional ball game—the depositions are just the warm-ups, not the real game. However, in our case, because David Hersh conducted an effective deposition, this warm-up time is what ended up winning the game for us.

While David was deposing one of fifteen potential witnesses whose responsibilities included monitoring flora, fauna, and flood damage on the Air Force Academy property, he reviewed photos of the accident site that the potential witness had on file.

One photo was of the accident site where I crashed on my bicycle. It was so clear that it appeared to be documentation after the fact. It would have been easy to skip to the next photo. However, David had a well-rehearsed process for depositions, and he followed it in detail. Despite the obvious nature of the photo, he asked the potential witness when he had taken the photo. When the answer was a date in August, weeks before my crash, our view of the entire case dramatically changed. If an Air Force representative knew of the damage weeks before my accident yet failed to take any corrective action or post any warnings, it meant that they were definitely at fault.

Although it still took several years to ensure the judges saw the facts in the right context relative to the laws, the entire outcome of my case hinged on that one simple question.

If you are dealing with a significant conflict, make sure you talk to the right people and find out the real details, even when it seems obvious what the story is.

Interesting Fact #1

During the deposition process for my trial, we learned that I was the third bicyclist injured at the same washed-out site. Although my injury was much more severe than the previous bicycle riders, that fact seemed to be all we would need to win the case. However, because the reports of injuries for the previous victims never reached the Air Force Academy, there was no benefit in bringing those facts against them before the court. It was a frustrating lesson to learn, but sometimes, even the best facts must be ignored, even in the most difficult situations.

Who Is the Judge?

Anytime we are dealing with a challenge or difficulty, many questions come to mind. Whether it's a relational problem, such as a divorce, a financial problem, such as bankruptcy, or a sickness or injury, questions like these pop up:

- Who caused the problem?
- Was it my error in judgment, or was someone else at fault?
- Should I have done something else?

When we start questioning things and talking to others about the possible answers, we're bound to get a variety of opinions. Some people might blame us, while others place no blame anywhere. So, whether litigation is involved or not, the underlying key factor is who makes the final decision. Who is the judge? Often, none of the answers are apparent quickly, and it may take some real time to determine the correct answers. Although the court may simplify and better define the process, this relates to many of the things we experience in our lives.

Our judge was a righteous man. I say he was "our" judge because the legal case was a joint lawsuit, filed on behalf of three parties. My case was the primary of the three. My wife Elizabeth also had a case for two reasons. When she first saw me with my injuries, she passed out and fell. She was injured and admitted to the hospital with me. Furthermore, as I mentioned, she had a significant loss of consortium due to my severe injuries. My medical insurance company also had a claim for repayment of their medical-related expenses if anyone was at fault.

Judge Daniel was randomly selected for our case in the District Court in the State of Colorado. Shortly after he was assigned the case, Judge Daniel retired. Fortunately, retiring judges often continue judging cases they have on their docket, even after they retire. It is the judge's choice whether to retain cases and which ones to retain. Fortunately, Judge Daniel, knowing our case, opted to continue to judge our case after his retirement.

Judge Daniel had to spend more time on our case than originally anticipated, but he stuck with it. After his first ruling, which found the USAFA liable, he held court to determine the damages that should be repaid. Then, after his decision was appealed, the circuit court of appeals remanded the case back to him to rule it under another law. When he again found in our favor, their appeal took it back to the circuit court of appeals.

Judge Daniel was a man who was easy to appreciate. He not only ruled in our favor, but he did everything he could to ensure he was making the right judgment. Although he didn't break any rules in his court, he made sure he got to the reality of the case. As an example, during the trial sitting to determine damages, the usual process is for the lawyers to ask all of the questions of the witnesses. The judge's job is to sit and listen, hearing the details the lawyers present through those witnesses.

In this second part of the trial, Judge Daniel didn't think he was hearing the bottom line based on the questions the lawyers were asking me, so when I was on the stand, he started asking me questions directly. In particular, after the doctor described the necessary surgical procedures expected to correct the damage to my jaw, Judge Daniel asked me if I would go through with that difficult and painful procedure. Based on my situation, I planned to go through the pain, and I let him know.

After we had been involved in the court process for years, once again we were back in front of Judge Daniel. He understood the pain we were going through due to the repeated appeals, so he ruled that the other side would be required to reimburse us for the legal costs associated with our case. Wherever there was a way for him to be fair, he went out of his way to do so.

As much as Judge Daniel cared about our case being ruled correctly, there was a sad note at the end of the case. After the second appeal, the Circuit Court of Appeals finally admitted they had ruled incorrectly on the first appeal. However, our opponents had ninety days to appeal to the US Supreme Court. Since that appeal was a possibility, we were still in an unknown state, waiting for the final verdict. We waited with bated breath, hoping they would not appeal, but we knew that could happen anytime until Monday, May 13, 2019. On that day, when they did not appeal, we knew Judge Daniel had indeed ruled correctly. Unfortunately, he passed away the Friday before—May 10. I am sure that, in heaven, he was glad to see that his ruling was upheld.

Often, you may believe you know whether you were right or wrong, but sometimes it takes a while to confirm it. Such was the case for us. With all of the appeals and reversals, it took ten additional judges nine years to fully confirm that Judge Daniel's original ruling was right. It's easy to complain about uncertainty and the slowness of the system, but if you focus on doing the right thing, you can trust the outcome will be good.

This reminds me of one time when Joe described to me how he had to wait for many years before others around him finally saw the reality he had experienced firsthand. He had to stand his ground, believing in what he knew to be true, even when everyone else doubted him.

The Legal Battle Ensues

You may have never been to court, except perhaps for jury duty or traffic court. I wish I could say that was true in my case. However, during all the time I spent in court, I learned so much more about the legal system than I ever anticipated. It turns out that, in general, there are two kinds of courts—criminal and civil. Since I was not accused of violating any laws, my trial would not be a criminal case.

In a civil case, the court's goal is to determine what damages should be collected by whom. In Colorado, as in many other states, there are state laws intended to protect us from one another, sometimes including limiting the risk of one person trying to take financial advantage of another who was trying to be helpful. In my case, Colorado had two laws that were designed to limit the liability of landowners. The two laws were similar, as both limited the liability a landowner could have if someone was injured on their property. So, although my case was civil, the court had to consider these laws. One of the critical things my lawyers had to consider at the beginning was how these two laws applied to my situation because we would file our suit on the basis of the laws.

In discussions with the Air Force Academy, their representatives often referred to me as a trespasser on their property. Based on that perception, my lawyers filed the suit as it related to the Colorado Premises Liability Act. Without going into all of the legal details, the key thing in my situation was that the landowner was only liable if they did *not* intend to allow me to recreate on their property. In other words, they would only be liable in my case if they considered me a trespasser. However, I would only be able to recover damages if the judge determined that I was an invitee or a licensee. This made my case a very narrow line to follow. In this case, the word *intend* becomes very significant, especially relating to the details involved. Although there was a fence around the property, with signs posted regularly that indicated people were not allowed to cross the fence line, there were also signs near the entrance of the property that warned against motorized vehicles using the road. The fact that there were openings built into the fence line at the property's edge seemed to indicate that it was okay to ride a bike on the paved road. However, in communications with the USAFA staff, they were adamant that I was a trespasser.

Everything ultimately comes down to the judge's ruling. With about fifty pages of details to document his ruling, the judge ruled that, because they considered me a trespasser, they did not have immunity to their liability. Since they were not immune, and because I was ruled to be both an invitee and a licensee, I was owed damages due to USAFA's liability under the Colorado Premises Liability Act. In addition, Elizabeth was owed payment for her damages, in her loss of consortium (benefits in a family relationship such as love, affection, companionship, etc.) because of my accident. The judge also found that I had no fault or negligence related to my accident.

We breathed a big sigh of relief as we heard this favorable judgment. The next step was to go back to court to determine what the USAFA's liability would cost them—the total dollar amount of the damages we experienced.

But then they appealed . . .

How Appealing Is This?

When we started going through the process of suing the Air Force Academy to determine their liability, it was very appealing for us to think about the size of the check we might receive to repay our extreme damages. However, it turns out that there is another meaning for the term *appeal* that did not have such a nice connotation for us. That type of appeal involves going to the appellate court, which is what the government did for the first time in 2014. Although it had already been six years since my crash, it turned out that the court battle was just beginning. During the next nine years, we would be in court four more times, dealing with their appeals. This was not "appealing" to our sense of confidence.

An appellate court reviews the decisions of a lower court to determine if there were legal errors that could affect the outcome of a case. Unlike a trial court, an appellate court does not hear witness testimony or examine new evidence. Instead, it focuses on reviewing the record from the trial court and the legal arguments presented in written briefs and, occasionally, oral arguments.

In many appellate courts, cases are heard by a panel of three judges. After hearing the case, the panel of judges deliberates privately. They discuss the legal issues, review the case record, and decide whether to affirm, reverse, or modify the lower court's decision. There is no set timeline for how quickly appellate judges must issue a ruling; it may take weeks or even months to thoroughly analyze the issues and write their opinion. This lack of a specific deadline allows the judges to give each case the careful attention it deserves, but it can also be frustrating for those involved. In our case, we experienced waiting times that ranged from a few months to longer than a year.

Dealing with Tough Times

The fall of 2016 was a challenging time to live through. When you are struggling and things keep not going your way, it can be difficult to know what to do; it is difficult to have hope. That's what that season was like for me. Many times, I felt like David battling a huge giant. The waiting was stressful and exhausting. Although we won in the district court, the other side's appeal took us to the Tenth Circuit Court of Appeals. Finally, after nine long months of waiting, the appeals court published their decision.

Although waiting that long was hard, the court's answer made us feel even worse. The court reversed part of the district court's decision and remanded it back to the district court to make another decision. It's hard to express our level of frustration when, after eight years of waiting and dealing with the courts, we would have to start over again. The reversal had to do with which law applied to our case. We had filed the suit under the Colorado Premise Liability Act, and the judge ruled that we should be paid damages based on his ruling under that law. However, the Circuit Court of Appeals ruled that the Colorado Recreational Use Statute applied instead. They ordered Judge Daniel to retry the case to specifically determine if the Air Force Academy was willful or malicious in its actions related to my case.

Once again, the legal meaning of a single word would determine the outcome of our case. This time the word was *willful*. Since the word *malicious* requires personal intent to harm a specific individual, the USAFA was not malicious toward me, but were they willful in their actions?

Usually, keywords are defined in the law where they are used, but not in my case. Unfortunately, Colorado did not have a legal definition for *willful* that applied, either. Judge Daniel had to research the whole country to determine what Colorado's definition of willful would be and determine how it applied in my case. This conundrum added stress to our waiting time.

As if that was not discouraging enough, the Department of Defense started threatening us. Although we had mediation sessions a couple of times over the years, those sessions were virtually meaningless. But since the Recreational Use Statute applied, we had to consider different rules contained in that law. One of the key differences was the opportunity it gave the judge to order the loser of the case to pay the winner's legal costs. That completely changed the possible financial outcomes for us in our case. Previously, since my crash, because our lawyers had taken the case on a contingent basis, the worst we could expect was to not receive payment for our damages. The government informed us that, if we lost, they would request the judge order us to reimburse their legal costs, which could amount to hundreds of thousands of dollars. Of course, they were hoping we would drop our case.

Our fears escalated. We were already sinking financially—would we have to face bankruptcy on top of everything else? To say our faith was sorely tested is an understatement. God had always provided for us, but the deck seemed stacked against us. Looking back, I'm not sure how we managed to live through that time. We persevered, though, because we believed strongly in the rightness of our case.

Thankfully, Judge Daniel's determination was in our favor, and it was well supported by his research and our arguments. He also awarded us reimbursement of our legal fees, which was even more encouraging.

But once again, an appeal was made.

It was tough continuing to wait for an answer for fourteen months, when, after the previous appeal, we heard in only three months.

Getting your day in court does not necessarily reflect how much preparation time and effort goes into getting to that point. It might refer to the actual time spent presenting a case, arguing a motion, or appearing before a judge, which might only take twenty minutes in the courtroom. However, what led to those twenty minutes was a significant amount of work—research, drafting legal documents, preparing arguments, and coordinating with clients and opposing parties. You might think of it like giving a twenty-minute speech that took days of work to prepare. The day in court phrase is a reminder that what happens in court is just the tip of the iceberg in the legal process.

The appellate process could have taken even longer. When the Circuit Court of Appeals ruled in our favor, the government had to decide whether to appeal that ruling to the US Supreme Court. Since they had up to ninety days to make that appeal, we were on pins and needles during that time. The circuit court gave its ruling in mid-February, and we had to wait until May to know if the verdict was real. Thankfully, our opponents did not appeal to the US Supreme Court, so we just had to wait for them to write the check.

Interesting Fact #2

After our trial was complete, we learned that the lawyer leading the opposition said he had never lost a case in his career, so it enhanced the idea that we were David going against Goliath. It also is interesting that, when he lost to us, he retired from practice. Sometimes, it does not matter what the reputation or strength of your opposition is—you can still be a victor.

Sadly, the kind of lengthy legal battle we endured is by no means uncommon. I can think of several that have been made into movies. For instance, *A Class Action* tells the story of the citizens of Woburn, Massachusetts, who brought a lawsuit against the owners of a food packaging plant for contaminating the city's water supply with carcinogens, which they believed caused at least six deaths from leukemia. That legal battle lasted four years, but in the end, the town won its case. Another example is the 2005 movie *North Country*, which stars Charlize Theron. She plays a female employee of an iron mine in northern Minnesota who speaks up on behalf of her fellow female employees regarding the extreme sexual harassment they endured from their male coworkers. She refused to give up even when fifty lawyers turned her down, but even when she finally found someone to represent her, the court proceedings were almost as bad as the harassment. After seven long years, the women of the mines were awarded $3.5 million.

There also have been some notable cases involving traumatic brain injuries—one man sued Mazda and won after he suffered a TBI due to a malfunctioning seat belt. Another case involved a gas station manager who experienced a TBI when a train derailed and careened into his office where he was sitting. His injury was so severe that he ended up needing long-term medical care, and the jury awarded him $60 million.

Malcolm Gladwell even wrote a book called *David and Goliath*, where he delves into "the art of battling giants." I'll end this chapter with a quote from his book.

What the Israelites saw, from high on the ridge, was an intimidating giant. In reality, the very thing that gave the giant his size was also the source of his greatest weakness. There is an important lesson in that for battles with all kinds of giants. The powerful and the strong are not always what they seem.[1]

1. Malcolm Gladwell, *David and Goliath: Underdogs, Misfits, and the Art of Battling Giants* (New York: Little, Brown and Company, 2013).

9

CHOOSING TO TRUST

*Trust God from the bottom of your heart; don't try to
figure out everything on your own. Listen for God's
voice in everything you do, everywhere you go;
he's the one who will keep you on track.*

During my lifetime, I've had many opportunities to trust—and each of them involved a choice on my part. Usually, fear was involved, and I would make a conscious decision to trust. We all face situations where we have to choose fear or trust—trusting a doctor who is recommending surgery, believing you'll find a job when you've just lost one, or having faith that you'll overcome a daunting situation.

One of the most memorable ones I've ever had was during my time in the Coast Guard when I was sailing on a tall ship. I didn't think consciously about trusting, but underneath it all, I was trusting a lot of things.

A tall ship is a large, traditionally rigged sailing vessel often associated with historical maritime adventures. These ships are characterized by their towering masts, expansive sails, and intricate riggings. To reach the sails, you must use ratlines—lengths of thin lines tied between the shrouds of a sailing ship to form a ladder. They're the equivalent of a ladder's steps, but not nearly as sturdy. With all the sailors going up and down to furl the sails, those ratlines wear out eventually. Especially toward the end of the season, a sailor could be climbing perhaps one hundred feet in the air, and one of those ratlines might give way, causing the sailor to lose his footing.

Therefore, we were always trained to have three points of contact on the ship's ropes. This meant we would use both hands and have at least one foot on something at all times. We would never want to put both feet on one ratline because, if it gave way, we'd find ourselves hanging by two hands. If we were only using one hand, we'd be hanging by one arm. How long could we hold on without falling?

So, we always held on to each side of the rope as we stepped with one foot on the ratline and carefully stepped on the next ratline with the other foot, slowly progressing that way until we reached the very top of the mast where there was just one ratline. As we climbed, the wind would blow and the rope ladder swayed—it was quite an experience.

It's a situation that demands a high level of trust—not only in God but in a bunch of people. We weren't thinking about this consciously, but when we were finally done docking the ship, we realized how much trust in fellow sailors was required and how thankful we were for their trustworthiness.

This is an extreme example, but if you stop to think about it, daily life requires a high degree of trust too.

- You trust that the food at the grocery store is safe to eat.
- You trust that, when you get on the road in your car, the brakes won't fail.
- You trust that gravity will keep you grounded.
- You trust that the sun will rise each morning.

Being Willing to Trust

Many times, our trust is based on an agreement. With our friends and colleagues, we trust the information we share with them will be safe, and that they will use it well. When we marry, we trust our spouse will honor their vows and stay with us for the rest of their lives. Obviously, spouses fail each other all the time and break that trust, but the point is that trust is based on a commitment.

The one person we can always trust to not fail us is God. When he makes a promise to us, it's almost like he's committing himself. We trust him to keep his word. When we look back at our lives, we can see evidence of his faithfulness and his goodness to us.

When my first marriage ended, I had to come to terms with the fact that we had both done things that hurt our relationship and destroyed our trust. Afterward, I had to decide if I would be willing to risk trusting again.

Then, one day I ran into Elizabeth, a woman I had known ten years before when we both lived in Stamford, Connecticut, and had gone to the same church. We both played on a coed softball team sponsored by the church. She got married and moved away, and my wife and I moved away from the area too.

But ten years later, we ran into each other at a church camp in New Hampshire. I had taken my daughter so she could hang out with her friends because she had worked at the church camp previously. We got there early enough to go to the chapel on Sunday morning. And at the end of the service, I saw Elizabeth sitting at the other end of the row.

I went over and said hello. She said hello and asked, "Where's Debbie?"

"She left," I said.

"Oh, is she in the bathroom?"

"No, she left *me*."

We decided to go for a walk before lunch, and we found a bench on the beach and sat and chatted. I knew she also had gone through a divorce.

"What are you going to do now?" I asked her.

"I've got to get back out West," she answered.

I hadn't realized she had lived in Arizona before Connecticut. And because I had grown up in Utah, I wanted to go back West too. A couple of years previously, I had told Debbie I thought we should move to Colorado Springs and raise our kids there. She wasn't open to that idea, so I thought, *Our marriage is more important*, and I didn't pursue it any further.

But when Elizabeth said, "I've got to get back West," it was like a light bulb went off. I suddenly realized I wasn't restricted anymore. I could go back West too. And so, I blurted out, "Well, don't leave without me!"

I wasn't proposing or anything, but I figured maybe we could help each other.

Soon after, I realized my boss was based in Colorado Springs although I was working in Connecticut where the headquarters were based. Even better, he wanted me to work with him out there. I could do that!

And six months later, we were married and relocated to Colorado. It was a great example of trusting that life is going to unfold the way it should.

Joe shared with me that he learned this when he was in a really bad situation. The way Joe trusted, even when falsely accused by his boss's wife, is an example of his strong faith and character. At the time, he was a servant in his boss's house. His boss trusted him so much that he put Joe in charge of everything he owned. However, the boss's wife tried to trick Joe into compromising his morals. When Joe refused because he wanted to stay faithful to God and loyal to his boss, she became angry. She lied, which led to Joe being thrown into prison even though he was innocent.

Instead of becoming bitter or giving up, my friend chose to

trust God. He believed God had a plan for him, even though his situation seemed unfair. While in prison, Joe continued to do his best; he continued to act with integrity and kindness, and God blessed him. He gained the trust of the prison warden and was eventually given responsibilities there too. Over time, God used Joe's faithfulness and trust to bring about something amazing—he was later released from prison and became a powerful leader in Egypt.

Joe's story teaches us that even when life feels unfair or others treat us badly, trusting in God and staying true to what is right can lead to blessings. If you want to learn more about Joe and all he went through, you can find his story in the pages of the Bible, where he's called Joseph.

Another Miraculous Opportunity to Trust

In 2020, I had another serious fall—this time, not off my bike but off a roof. Finally, after eleven years, we received the damage reimbursement from the bike crash, and I was free financially, so I quit my job. My brother was building a house in Utah, and I decided to go to Utah and help him put a roof on the house.

I was working on a section of the roof when the support cleat gave way and I fell. When I hit the ground, I broke my neck. A vertebrae facet cracked but it didn't break off. I had to wear a neck brace for three months. If I hadn't hit something or caught onto something, I might have broken my neck fatally and died. Instead, I caught on a nail. My scalp was ripped open from my eyelid to the crown of my head, and I eventually needed 120 stitches. My scalp was lying on the side of my head. Amazingly, there were no additional injuries to my brain.

But the real miracle is something that happened several years before that. At some point—I'm not sure if I was asleep or awake—I had a vision. In the vision, I was helping my brother work on the roof of his house, and I saw myself falling. It was very vivid, and in my dream, I asked God, "Is this really going to happen?" I didn't get an answer, but a couple of times that year, I would remember the vision and ask God if it was going to happen. I never got an answer and, eventually, I forgot about it.

What made the vision strange was that, at the time I saw it, I lived in Colorado, and my brother lived in Delaware. He had been living there for ten or fifteen years running a business. It seemed unlikely that I would ever go to Delaware to help him with his roof. But then his circumstances changed, and he moved back to Utah. He started building a log house—in the middle of winter. He told me he was trying to finish putting a metal roof on his new house, and that was when I made the six-hour drive to his house to help him.

That morning, we had gone to church. When we got home, we started on the second half of the roof. The roof was at a forty-five-degree angle, and the edge of the roof was twelve feet above the ground.

To make sure the front edge of the roof was aligned perfectly, we had to measure precisely. The cleat I was standing on was in the way of doing the measurements, so I moved it. But I must not have done it properly because when I was on it, it gave way. On my way down, I caught another cleat and went through that. My brother was on a ladder and saw me fall. He was tempted to try and stop me, but he knew that, if he did, we both would go down.

I hit the ground, and I immediately thought, *Yep, it's really going to happen.* Instantly, my vision from several years before came back to me in vivid detail. In my vision, I knew Josh, my brother's son, would be coming pretty quickly, and he would get me ready for the ambulance. Unbeknownst to me, when my brother had lived in Delaware, Josh had been a top EMT.

Sure enough, Josh arrived home from church, saw what had happened, and was able to get me ready for the ambulance, which got there a few minutes later.

My brother has almost 500 acres of property and lives ten miles from the nearest town, so it helped that Josh was able to help prep me before the paramedics arrived. When they got there, they didn't have to do anything except put me in the ambulance.

In my vision, I had seen two women in the ambulance, and sure enough, both nurses were women. They rushed me to the little hospital in a town of 10,000 residents near where my brother lived. The medical staff was so impressive. It was incredible what a great job they did for being such a small hospital. They were doing such a fantastic job that I wasn't sure the next part of my vision would happen because, in my vision, I had to be transported to another hospital.

When I hit the ground, within thirty seconds my phone rang. It was Elizabeth calling because, while she had been in church, she suddenly had a strong sense that something was wrong. She thought, *I need to leave and call Jim* now.

So, she left church and called me, but when I heard her name on the caller ID, I quickly told my brother, "Don't answer it."

After not answering her first call, a couple of hours later while I was lying in the emergency room, she called again, and I answered the phone. When she asked me where I was, I said, "Well, I'm on a gurney." Pretty quickly she realized I was at the hospital, not on the job site.

"I told you not to go on the roof!" she said. When she realized the extent of my injuries, she added, "I don't want you looking like Frankenstein, so make sure the surgeon knows what he's doing when he stitches you up." After examining me and consulting with his team, the surgeon said, "Okay, this is beyond us. We've got to send him to Provo."

They put me back in the ambulance for the ninety-minute ride to Provo. While they stitched me up, Eric was able to watch, and he counted each of the 120 stitches they used to reattach my scalp. Although it may sound strange, I suspect he was glad there were not more stitches than that as he did not want me to pass him in our lifetime stitches competition.

With that ride, another part of my vision had come to pass.

My brother and his wife Trish had been involved in reviving a church in Price when they moved to Utah. It was still very small, and they were struggling to get it up and thriving. My brother ended up becoming the pastor of that little congregation. As they were building the house, they were living in an RV during a very cold winter. There were many times when they asked themselves, "Is this really what we're supposed to be doing?" But when Trish heard about my vision, it became clear that God's hand was in it, and it renewed her motivation to persevere and keep going.

I was in a neck brace for three months, but other than that I had no ill effects. It was miraculous, really. The facet is a little triangular-shaped bone that protrudes and nerves run through it. My facet joint was cracked, but because it didn't break off, by wearing the neck brace, it healed in place.

Crisis or God Working?

Let's change the time frame and go back a few thousand years. According to the standard carnal perspective, a guy called Joe got dumped by his brothers and was sold as a slave. Being a slave was terrible, but from there he was thrown in jail. I know this is hard to imagine, but while in jail, the guys he had been with forgot about him. Sounds like pretty bad news, right? Would that be considered a crisis in your life?

The amazing reality about this situation was that God's hand was able to work through the events, and one result was that Joe (a.k.a. Joseph) was able to save his family from a famine. God also used those events and that salvation to move the family of only seventy people to a secure place where they could live and thrive and turn into a nation of millions. That nation, God has used for millennia to heal and do His work in the world.

I am amazed at the reality of Joe's crisis and now have a different perspective on the "accident" I experienced. I've wondered when Joe started thanking God for the situation— when he was thrown in the pit, sold as a slave, tossed in prison, or ever? When I asked him, he told me, "All of the above!"

Because of the insight God has given me through the history of Joe and others over the years, I can share the many ways he has answered prayer and made me even better than I was before the crash. That list is growing continuously, especially while I follow Joe's example and focus on serving God each step of the way. Praise God!

Unexpected Gifts

Isn't it wonderful to receive a gift you did not expect—one that isn't related to any special event, one you never even asked for? It might not happen often, but when it does, it's a real blessing. Here is a story about an unexpected gift I received.

Several months after my crash and release from the hospital, I was chatting with my brother Eric. I described my total lack of motivation or interest in doing anything. "I'm just so frustrated," I told him.

Eric then told me he'd had a similar experience. Although he is my brother and we've always gotten along well, we've never made it a practice to have regular conversations. At that time, he was running a business in Delaware and focused on building it, so he typically didn't have time for random chats. In addition, since he is ten years younger than me, our families have always been in different stages of life. Thankfully, though, on that particular day, he shared with me what he had lived through three years earlier.

As is often the case in Delaware (and is true in many other northeastern states), ticks and tick-borne diseases have become a real issue. Because he worked outdoors, Eric was often bitten by ticks; it just went with the territory. However, in 2006, one particular tick infected him with a rare disease called Ehrlichiosis. Records show that during that year, there were only 250 cases of Ehrlichiosis nationally. (My brother and I have a family habit of subjecting ourselves to unusual maladies.)

After Eric was bitten by the tick, the symptoms of the disease showed up within a day, resulting in a high fever of 106 degrees that lasted for five days. Fortunately, the hospital was able to keep him alive, and he was able to go back to operating his service business. Unfortunately, he soon lost all motivation and desire to do all the tasks needed to keep his employees busy and his family fed. As the boss, when you are on your own in that kind of situation, you are really on your own.

He had a team of good doctors, though. One of his doctors checked his hormones and found that his testosterone level was extremely low. The normal level for his age would have been 250 or higher, but his was under twenty. His lack of testosterone was causing a lack of motivation. When he got replacement testosterone through a series of regular shots, his motivation returned.

Eric thought I should get my testosterone level checked, and his story gave me hope, so I decided it was a good idea. However, at that time, I had a couple of things working against me. Good idea or not, my lack of motivation ensured that I wasn't going to go out of my way to do anything. I was so tired of going to doctors and dentists that I had put a personal limit of having no more than one doctor or dentist visit per week. So, it took a while, but finally, when my next regular blood test was scheduled, I asked my doctor to include testosterone.

Of course, it was no surprise that the results showed that my testosterone level was low. My doctor said I would need to see an endocrinologist, who would determine the therapy I'd need. In our area, endocrinologists were in short supply, but once again, my lack of motivation kicked in, and I dragged my feet about making an appointment. More time passed, and when I finally called the endocrinologist's office, they said it would be five months or longer before they could see me as a new patient. Talk about disappointing! *Am I ever going to get my motivation back?* I wondered. I felt more depressed than ever and very discouraged.

But one day, when I was at my doctor's office for yet another visit, a woman behind me in line heard me telling the nurse about my struggle, and she let me know that her husband had just been through a similar challenge but found an endocrinologist who was available in Denver. That would involve a drive of over an hour, but it was worth the drive. I had learned my lesson; I made a call to his office right away, and I was able to book an appointment to see him in two weeks.

When I finally saw the endocrinologist, his diagnosis was very detailed. He said my condition was both rare and severe. After another brain scan, he confirmed that, during my crash, my brain was rattled hard enough to break my pituitary.

The doctor explained that our pituitary gland controls all of the other glands in our body, and since mine was broken, it was no longer giving orders to the other glands. To rectify it, the endocrinologist prescribed replacement hormones that I would have to take for the rest of my life.

One in a Million

Over and over again, my accident has allowed me to be knowledgeable about things I never wanted to know. I am thankful, though, that much of this knowledge has not been useless, as I have been able to help others because of what I have learned. One example is what I now know about the pituitary gland. It's a very important gland as it controls many other glands in the body, including testosterone levels. This means that, even if your glands can produce testosterone, without the pituitary giving direction, nothing happens. That was my problem.

It turned out that my case was pretty rare. One day during my visit, the endocrinologist commented that it was a very unusual day because I was one of two patients he saw who suffered from something called panhypopituitarism. It is very rare, affecting about one in every 500,000 people. He also explained that most of those who suffer from it develop it due to cancer or surgery. The fact that I had contracted it from a traumatic brain injury meant I was really "one in a million." Usually, most of us want to be that unusual by winning the lottery or some other good thing. I may not be excited to be that rare, but I am very thankful to have survived it.

The good news was that I regained some of my motivation, but the bad news was the human growth hormone (HGH) replacement meant I had to give myself an expensive shot in my belly every night . . . forever. Compared to the alternatives, I was thankful modern medicine was able to provide such amazing therapies, but it didn't mean I liked paying the price.

Through the years, I've learned much more about endocrinology, and I've been able to help advise others with similar symptoms. The doctor told me my condition rarely is cured, but if it is, it's always within a year or two of its beginning. I accepted that this was now a part of my life, and I expected to deal with it as long as I lived.

One morning, I was sharing this with a small group at church when we were telling one another about the medical things we were dealing with. A week later, Terri, one of the women who had been in the small group, came to me with an unusual statement. She told me that God had directed her to pray for my pituitary to be healed. She told God she would, and I was very appreciative of her direction and obedience. It left me a little confused, though. I believed God could heal my pituitary, but how would I recognize the healing? It was not like a blind man who could now see or a lame man who could now walk; my disability was not visually evident.

Since my endocrinologist was a leading authority in the field, I asked her how she might confirm that my pituitary had been healed. I was hoping to hear good news soon. Imagine my disappointment when she said it would take six months to confirm such a healing. But I was thrilled when six months had passed, and she was able to confirm my pituitary was working again. I was free of expensive daily shots, and I could live the rest of my life with more freedom than I had imagined. I am so thankful for this gift that I never asked for.

When my buddy Joe ended up in Egypt, his life didn't look like it was full of blessings. After being falsely accused of rape, he spent a few years in prison. But then God did something unexpected for Joe. He gave him the ability to explain the strange dreams Pharoah had been having. He told Pharoah there would be seven years of plenty, followed by seven years of famine. Pharoah was so grateful that he appointed Joe to a high office, placing him in charge of the food supplies. Joe received an unexpected gift when things looked pretty bleak for him.

When the famine hit, back in Canaan, Joe's family was struggling. They made their way to Egypt where Joe saw to it that they were taken care of. He was able to offer his brothers an unexpected gift too, thus passing on the protection and provision he had received from God.

What a great God we have! Keep your eyes open—there are blessings all around us.

Early Miracles

As you've learned, I've had my share of brain injuries. I've told the story of my first concussion and breaking the back of my skull when I was three or four. But throughout the years, I had other head injuries too. Once, I was playing on a swing set and banged my head hard against a bar that had something sticking out of it. When I was in college in Connecticut, I learned how to ski, so as a sophomore at the Coast Guard Academy, I went skiing with my sister. She had never skied before, and I offered to teach her. At one point, I was skiing backward down the hill, snowplowing, so I could tell her what to do. Everything was going fine until I fell over backward and hit my head. I tried to get up, but I kept falling over, so the ski patrol had to take me back down to the lodge. I had no memory of that week, and the next year when we went back to that resort, and I had no memory of being there at all.

It's pretty interesting because all the injuries I've had throughout my lifetime have all been significant head injuries. Many times, I've wondered why God has kept me here through all my various accidents. I know he must have a reason. My sister knew of someone who was working on a roof and had a much less serious fall than I did, and that person died. But I survived. It motivates me to tell God, "You've obviously got me here for a reason. It would be nice to know what it is, but I don't have to know either."

The fact that I'm still alive after going through so many medical events and treatments makes me believe God's hand is in all of it. I'm always open to sharing my knowledge and understanding with others who have similar medical issues.

As you reflect on your own life, what situations have you lived through that have given you wisdom you can share with others? Nothing that happens to us is wasted; God always has a purpose for us, and, often, what looks like the worst case can be used to console and bless others in their trials. You never know how your story might impact someone else, and you might never know if it did, but keep sharing from your heart, trusting God will use you.

10

THE FUTURE LOOKS BRIGHT

I know what I am doing. I have it all planned out—plans to take care of you, not abandon you, plans to give you the future you hope for.

Yes to Requests

I enjoy helping people and doing things for others. I've been fascinated at times with the various ways people make their requests when they want something done. For instance, someone might ask, "How would you feel about taking out the trash?" After hearing that many times, I finally realized the person asking the question did not honestly care how I felt about taking out the trash; they just wanted the task done and preferably done *now*. That style is similar to the question that begins with "How would you like to . . . ?" When you are programmed like me, as an engineer, to understand things literally, it is hard to know sometimes whether the person asking the question wants to know if I would like to do this, or if they are making a request.

Similarly, God can make requests of us in many different

ways. Over the years, I have found that the more I pay attention to these requests, the better the results are for me, as well as for others. One weekend retreat, a couple of years before my crash, provides a good example.

During the small group times that weekend, my friend Brad went through a time of revival and recommitted his life to Christ. As a follow-up to the retreat, we sensed God was asking us to start a small group of men who would meet weekly to provide one another with spiritual support, encouragement, and accountability. That group has met consistently for more than eighteen years, has outlived the church that started it, and includes three generations of men who range in age from twenties to eighties.

The men at that retreat each heard requests from God in different ways. But because Brad and I stepped up to do what we heard God asking us to do, the results have been life-changing.

No Coincidences

That retreat was a powerful experience in other ways too. While my dad and I planned to participate in the retreat, our primary purpose for being there was to spend time together. When we got there and signed in, we were disappointed when we found out we had a roommate. It would surely disrupt the time we had available to talk and pray together. *Oh well*, I thought, *we'll deal with it.*

Our roommate was Wayne Gage, a man from our church I didn't know well. Ironically, he was dealing with a minor disappointment as well. Usually, when he attended any event, God gave him an "assignment" of someone he was to help. Being an experienced medical doctor, there were many ways he might help someone. But that time he had no sense of who he was there to help. Well, he was there, and so were we, all making the best of our situations.

At the retreat, we made some good memories. Dad and I had each learned how to play Sudoku, and we were able to enjoy playing games together. Watching us, Wayne was impressed with how we enjoyed our time together, even with such a simple pastime. We also enjoyed participating in the small group discussion times we had during the weekend. It provided times for us, as men, to get to know one another better and to learn from Scripture.

It turned out that it was a blessing my dad was able to make it to the retreat that weekend. He had consistently been experiencing suicidal thoughts, even on the several-hour drive to the retreat. Every time he met a tractor-trailer truck on the highway, he was tempted to swerve and drive into the front of the truck, killing himself. He didn't like having to live with that intense temptation, but he had been dealing with it for some time.

During the weekend, Dad shared his struggle with me, and Wayne also learned what he was dealing with. Wayne heard a calling to pray for the healing of Dad's mental temptation. His prayer was answered quickly as Dad reported he was able to make the drive home with no temptations. In a very unusual way, Dr. Wayne Gage saved my dad's life, giving him many more years to live. Dad is now in his ninetieth year and has lived for decades without suicidal temptations.

After my bicycle crash, I was thankful to have Dr. Gage available as a trusted friend to provide second opinions on the many medical issues I dealt with due to my severe TBI.

A Life of Imitating Others

Imitation gets a bad rap. We shun phoniness; we value

authenticity. We don't want imitation anything; we want the real deal. But could imitation be a good thing?

Imitation can be valuable for learning, growth, and mastery. By studying and mimicking the techniques of experts, we can develop new skills and deepen our understanding of a craft. In art, music, and writing, imitation often serves as a foundation for creativity, helping individuals absorb styles and techniques before developing their own unique voices. In business and innovation, imitation can improve upon existing ideas, making them more efficient or accessible. Even in personal development, observing and emulating admirable traits in others can help shape positive habits. When used as a stepping stone rather than a substitute for originality, imitation can be a powerful means of progress.

One of the games I remember playing as a child had a song associated with it, and it turns out it also had some significant life lessons associated with it as well. To play Follow the Leader, one kid was the leader, and the rest of the kids followed while attempting to do exactly what the leader did. If the leader spun in a clockwise circle, you did that as well. If they somersaulted, you tried to do an identical one. If you weren't able to imitate the person at the front of the line, you had to go to the back of the line and start over again.

It was a fun game, and we did it while singing this chorus:

"Following the leader, the leader, the leader. We're following the leader wherever he may go."

If you turn this childhood game into a lifestyle question— "Who are you following?"—you quickly realize it's important to choose a good leader to follow, since they determine where you will end up going. Going a little further, I realize that Follow the Leader effectively creates an *imitation chain*. A chain is a connected flexible series of links that are used to pull a load. When I add the adjective *imitation* to it, it makes me think of two possibilities.

1. A decorative paper chain—This is an imitation because it looks like a chain but cannot move a significant load. In this imitation chain, the whole thing is a fake. It's great for decoration, but it doesn't function as a real chain.

2. A steel chain—If each link in the chain is an imitation of the link before it, they can all work together to move a heavy load. In this imitation chain, each link can be a good imitation of the link before it, making a strong chain. I used a chain with my truck to pull a garbage truck when it was stuck in the mud while my house was under construction. If any of the links in that chain were poor imitations, the chain would not have been able to do the job like it did.

A chain is only as strong as its weakest link. Don't be that person!

Many years ago, at another retreat, the speaker asked a question I've never forgotten: "What kind of old man do you want to be?" I was a young man at the time, and I had never really considered this before, but that question got my attention. As I continued to think about it, I realized that whatever habits I practiced and whoever I imitated during the coming years would largely determine who I was when, and if, I lived to be an old man.

It was probably around that time of my life that I started repeating the phrase, "I want to be like my dad when I grow up." Now, being a grown-up is very subjective; it's a concept I believe always applies no matter what our age. Essentially, it asks the question, "Who do I want to be later in my life?" Because of the kind of person my dad was and how he treated others, I wanted to imitate him—and that is still the case today.

After my crash, I realized I had made much progress in my goal of "being like my dad." In addition to all the physical changes I had to deal with as a result of my accident, there were also changes in my personality. I found that I was acting much more like my dad on a day-to-day basis. In talking about the crash, I often said, "I got twenty years older that day"—not because of physical aging but because of how much better I imitated my dad, who is about twenty years my senior.

Before my crash, as an engineer, my personality was very purpose-driven. If I didn't have a defined purpose for a conversation, I wouldn't waste my time starting one. My dad was different. He would frequently chat with strangers just to be friendly. After my TBI, that became my practice as well. I went from purpose-driven conversations to spontaneous ones, and I was often surprised at the unexpected benefits I gained from those conversations. Someone might say something randomly that provided me with a new insight or a new connection.

As I have passed the three-score year mark in my life, I have realized this imitation chain I am a part of not only has links I am following like my dad but there are links following me. I hope the links who are imitating me are strong and are helping move the load in the right direction. I want to be able to say what the Apostle Paul boldly and confidently told the early church in Corinth, "Imitate me, as I imitate Christ."

We all have a choice. Who will we imitate, and how well will we imitate them?

On Trusting Others

Trust. Now that is a tough word. What does it mean to trust in someone or something? If I trust in something, does that always include a person or the people behind it?

Trust seems to be the antonym of fear. If a situation might make me fear, some level of trust should reduce or remove that fear from my psyche. However, does a certain level of trust always result in success or safety? Here are some thoughts about my experiences relating to types of trust.

I had a memorable experience while sailing across the Atlantic Ocean from Spain as a teenager. Many types of trust could be inferred from that experience. One day, while under sail over a thousand miles from the coast, I decided to climb to the top of the mainmast of the tall ship on which I was being trained. The climb up the mast took me 150 feet above the water, which would have been a very long fall.

At that moment, who was I trusting?

- The commanding officer and his navigator—that they were taking us back to our home country?
- The helmsman—that he would keep the ship going with the wind to not ruffle the sails and blow me off the mast?
- The boatswain mate who tied the rigging well enough that the ratlines would not break under my weight?

I am sure I could continue making a much more complete list of my trust, but you get the point; there were many people and related things that required my trust.

One of my trust questions is this: Was my safe ascent and descent to the top of this high mast due to my trust? It may have been, but it was also due to my training and trust in myself to behave a certain way.

Later in my Coast Guard career, I had the opportunity to con a ship into a port call on a fast-flowing river in Michigan. Due to the details of the situation that day, I had the will and the way to dock the ship quickly. Without going into too many details, the typical method of docking the ship was to turn around carefully in the middle of the river, slowly creep to the berth, and put the lines over while maneuvering in close.

However, on that day, I took the initiative to try and dock the ship quickly since we had been out of port for several days, and we all wanted to get home. I made a big U-turn, using much of the width of the river to do so. To accomplish that maneuver, I had to use commands I had never used before, such as ordering the helmsman to use hard-rudder rather than the usual smaller rudder commands. At the same time, I pushed the engine control to full power to get the ship to turn quickly in the strong current.

Thankfully, my ship handling was successful, and I did not ground the ship. Afterward, I learned more about the trust I was relying on during that maneuver. The engineer let me know he was in the engine room at the time and had disabled the governor on the engine while I was making the ship go to full power. He indicated that my commands would have tripped the engine offline, resulting in a grounding on the riverbank we were headed toward, or worse.

In that situation, I would describe my trust as coming from my ignorance. Being a deck officer, I had no clue as to the stresses or challenges I might be putting the ship and its crew through, but I trusted and took action anyway.

Optimism Is the True Moral Courage

Another one of my heroes is Ernest Shackelton. He is best known not for his achievements or his success but for his leadership and the way he dealt with adversity. He was able to inspire optimism in those around him when facing incredible odds. Here are four of my favorite Shackelton quotes:

- The quality I look for most is optimism: especially optimism in the face of reverses and apparent defeat. Optimism is true moral courage.
- To be brave cheerily, to be patient with a glad heart, to stand the agonies of thirst with laughter and song, to

walk beside death for months and never be sad—
that's the spirit that makes courage worth having.

- Men are not made from easy victories but based on great defeats.
- If you're a leader, a fellow that other fellows look to, you've got to keep going.

Back in 1914, Shackelton and his crew of twenty-seven were sailing to Antarctica, hoping to reach the South Pole, but they ended up getting caught in some ice, where they were trapped in the stormiest of seas for the next seventeen months. Eventually, Shackelton took seven of the men in a lifeboat on a journey of 850 miles where they finally found help. The amazing thing was that none of the twenty-seven crew members died. He was an awesome leader, and in the face of such adversity, he was able to stay calm and motivate his crew to do the same. I've endeavored to live my life by his same philosophy, and I know it's served me well in the face of my own seemingly insurmountable challenges.

Honoring Others

Experiencing a near-fatal crash as I did and surviving it provides an eye-opening perspective on life and relationships. It makes you think about what matters most and *who* matters most. Although I have not done it very often, I believe it is a good idea to look at our relationships occasionally and evaluate them. Healing from my accident gave me the time, space, and perspective to think about my relationships. As I evaluated them, I thought about what action, if any, I should take based on the results of my analysis.

- Are my relationships good or bad, beneficial or costly, significant or worthless?
- Should a particular relationship be enhanced or terminated?
- Should I honor the other person in my relationship?

If we honor someone, it means we regard them with great respect. This led to more questions.

- Who do we honor and how?
- At what cost do we honor them?
- Is there a benefit to honoring them?

As I considered this topic further, I realized there are very few people who I have taken any action to honor in my lifetime —either due to their position or their performance or both. I'll tell you about a few of them.

One group of people we are called to honor regardless of their performance is our parents. Most people who deserve honor due to their organizational position get that honor by our obedience. And as children, we honor our parents by obeying them. However, as God calls us to honor our fathers and mothers, when we reach adulthood, it is not as simple as doing what they ask. With that dilemma, and given the distance between Utah and Connecticut, I struggled to find a way to honor my parents once I was an adult with my own children.

One year, I had the idea that I could honor them by calling them each weekend to talk despite the cost of a long-distance phone call. The first time I called, they were glad to get the call. As time went on, they enjoyed getting regular phone calls from me, even though they didn't know my real reason for calling. I continued that habit for several years. But then I had the crash, and my TBI caused me to forget about making those regular weekend calls. After a couple of months, my dad mentioned how much they missed my calls, and I once again began calling them each week.

Several months after my crash, I met a friend of a friend who offered me a deeper understanding of why I was still alive after such a serious trauma. She pointed out that God's request (command) to honor our parents is also the first commandment with a promise attached to it. The fourth commandment says we should honor our fathers and mothers so we will "live long in the land." Since I was about to turn fifty, God granted me additional years of life because I had continued to honor my parents. I am thankful my parents were good parents; they deserved my honor based on their performance. But no matter what kind of parents we have, I also believe we will be rewarded if we find a way to honor our parents based on God's request.

Giving Back

I mentioned earlier in the book the way R.G. LeTourneau turned disappointment into opportunity, and here's another part of his story that has inspired me. He became very successful, receiving more than 300 patents for his inventions in the construction industry. His profits were in the millions, and back then, in the 1920s and 1930s, that was a lot of money. But he and his wife lived simply and always gave generously to missions and Christian education, even starting an engineering college. By the end of his life, he was giving away 90 percent of his earnings. He and his wife lived on the remaining 10 percent—and they lived quite well on that 10 percent. This drove home the lesson for me that you can't out-give God!

Leaving a Legacy

What have you inherited? Most people's answer to that question is, "Nothing yet," because their parents have not died and left them any material possessions. However, I like to expand the term *inheritance* a little beyond the money that might be handed down. Your inheritance might include things like your eye color, mental ability, physical strength, financial acuity, attitudes, and personality traits.

The more I look at my own experiences and family history, the more I am thankful for all I have inherited. Having to deal with the aftermath of my crash, I'm thankful I inherited from my parents the attitude that I was going to do whatever I could to recover as much as possible. I wasn't going to claim disability or waste my life blaming someone else for my difficulties. In the pages of this book, I hope I have been able to pass on some of this attitude to you, and I hope my story inspires you to meet your challenges with faith in God's protection and providence.

Take your everyday, ordinary life—your sleeping, eating, going-to-work, and walking-around life—and place it before God as an offering. Embracing what God does for you is the best thing you can do for him.

ABOUT THE AUTHOR

Author Jim Nelson grew up in Moab, Utah. He attended the United States Coast Guard Academy. After serving in the Coast Guard, he had a career of facilities management, which included management of buildings for GE, Hartford Public Schools, Johnson Controls, Pfizer, United Rentals, AIMCO, YMCA, and Pikes Peak Library District.

He helped raise eight children and is thankful for each of the sixteen grandchildren they have blessed him with so far.

If you have interest in Jim's waffles, in learning more about TBIs, light therapy, LearningRx, or hearing more of his testimony, feel free to contact him at Jim.PPP@bikerider.com.

BrainRX Locations

LearningRX Locations